26-18120

BX 153.E6

THE OLDEST CHRISTIAN PEOPLE

THE MACMILLAN COMPANY
NEW YORK · BOSTON · CHICAGO · DALLAS
ATLANTA · SAN FRANCISCO

MACMILLAN & CO., LIMITED
LONDON · BOMBAY · CALCUTTA
MELBOURNE

THE MACMILLAN CO. OF CANADA, LTD.
TORONTO

THE OLDEST CHRISTIAN PEOPLE

A Brief Account of the History and Traditions of the Assyrian People and the Fateful History of the Nestorian Church

by

WILLIAM CHAUNCEY EMHARDT
K. S. S. (*Greece*) K. S. H. S. (*Jerusalem*)
Secretary for Europe and Near East of the
National Council of the Episcopal Church

AND

GEORGE M. LAMSA
A Native of Kurdistan (Assyria) and Field
Representative of the American Branch of the
Archbishop of Canterbury's Assyrian Mission

Introduction by
RT. REVEREND JOHN GARDINER MURRAY
Presiding Bishop of the
Protestant Episcopal Church of America
1926

New York
THE MACMILLAN COMPANY
1926

All rights reserved

Copyright, 1926,
By THE MACMILLAN COMPANY

Set up and electrotyped.
Published October, 1926.

Printed in the United States of America by
THE FERRIS PRINTING COMPANY, NEW YORK.

To
MRS. WM. M. WOOD
of
BOSTON

CONTENTS

CHAPTER		PAGE
I.	THE REMNANT OF THE ASSYRIANS	19
II.	ASSYRIAN TRADITIONS	23
III.	THE EVANGELIZATION OF THE ASSYRIANS	37
IV.	ROMAN AND PERSIAN WARS	44
V.	NESTORIUS AND THE ASSYRIANS	49
VI.	NESTORIAN CUSTOMS AND PRACTICES	57
VII.	NESTORIAN MISSIONS IN THE FAR EAST	64
VIII.	RISE OF ISLAM AND THE ARABIAN CONQUEST	74
IX.	RELATION BETWEEN CHRISTIANS AND MOHAMMEDANS	80
X.	THE ADVENT OF THE WESTERN MISSIONS IN THE EAST	89
XI.	DURING THE WAR	107
XII.	THE ASSYRIANS SINCE 1918	115
XIII.	THE ASSYRIANS BEFORE THE LEAGUE OF NATIONS	121
XIV.	FINAL SETTLEMENT	130
	Postlude	135
	Bibliography	137
	Index	139

PREFACE

We must look to the Biblical records for the most picturesque portrait and accurate information relative to the history and power of the ancient Assyrian Empire. Yet it was not until 1842, when M. Botta, the French Consul at Mosul, discovered the long buried Assyrian cities, temples, relics, and chronological records, that the world knew of the highly developed civilization which had once existed in the Mesopotamian desert. M. Botta's discoveries also included the magnificent palace of the Emperor Sargon at Khorsabad, built 1722 B.C. This discovery has stimulated interest in further search for other long lost treasures.

Thanks are due to Sir Henry Rawlinson for his most valuable service in finding the keys of the Assyrian language and deciphering ancient codes and texts. Since these discoveries were made, scholars have been translating Assyrian tablets and throwing light upon ancient history as well as upon the history of religion.

The word Assyrian is derived from the Aramaic word "Ashur," which comes from the word "Athra" (land). Even today some of the Assyrian tribes use "sh" for "t." Ashur, which means landlord, is often used as the name of Assyrian kings, just as the Indian "Maharajah" is, which also means the owner of the land. Furthermore, Ashur is also used to refer to God. While the Bible states that Ashur was the son of Shem (Gen. x.22),

PREFACE

the Hebrew name for Assyria is "Beth-nahreen," the land of the rivers, and the Arabs called it "Athrar-Al-Jezira," the island. Ethnologically, the Assyrians were one of the divisions of the Semitic race who spoke Aramaic. Abraham was an Assyrian who crossed the River Euphrates, seeking grass and better opportunities in Canaan. Hence, his descendants, the Hebrews, were called by the Assyrians "Abar," from the Aramaic word "to cross." Philologically, Aramaic is the source of the dialects spoken by the various Semitic tribes. It is not only the language which Christ spoke, but the language also, we are told, which God spoke to Adam. During the Grecian conquest of the Near East it was the universal speech and continued to be until the thirteenth century. At present the language is spoken only by the very small group of Assyrians who have maintained their old traditions and their racial identity in the fastnesses of Kurdistan.

The hiatuses in the history of the present Assyrians and their racial identity have been puzzling, not only to leading scholars, but even to Assyrians. From the downfall of the Assyrian Empire, 610 B.C., until the present time, the history of the remnant of the Assyrian race has been very obscure. Some scholars still call them Syrians, others claim that they are the lost tribes of Israel, carried into captivity by the Assyrian Kings. Those who have made searching investigation have finally decided to class them as the remnant of the old Assyrian race. Recent history throws very little light on the subject. Whatever conclusions scholars may reach, the fact should not be ignored that the natives of this land have always maintained their racial and cultural identity with the ancient Assyrians. There is abundant material, written and legendary, showing the continuity of the race.

INTRODUCTION

The interest shown by the last four archbishops of Canterbury in the preservation of the ancient Assyrian (Nestorian) Church is sufficient evidence of the importance this little Church holds in the eyes of Christian leaders. History justifies this assumption. That the Church is strategically placed and traditionally endowed for an important mission in the Near East cannot be doubted. Semitic in its origin and traditions, approaching the Persian with an understanding born of close association for millenniums, almost indigenous in India, and filled with a missionary spirit, favored by special recognition by the Prophet Mohammed, this little Church seems the natural organization for producing prophets to the Mohammedan world.

The writers of this book endeavor to trace in outline the rise and fall of the ancient Church of Assyria. We are told of the founding of a Church among people speaking the language our Lord spoke, who found in Him the fulfillment of those prophecies which the calamitous experiences of the Hebrew had made current in Mesopotamia, as well as Syria and Palestine. We follow the Church in its effort to preserve the integrity of the faith in its simplicity. Their triliteral language was not capable of expressing the subtle distinctions of Greek philosophical thought, upon which the more analytic theology of the West is based. The period of missionary development challenges our attention and evokes our admiration. We grieve as the Tamerlane draws over this ancient Church and people the darkening shadow of oppression and decline.

Confined at last to their mountain fastnesses, the little remnant continue steadfast in the faith. Trial, suffering, abundant opportunity to prosper through apostasy, has left them unshaken. They are not a gentle people, but their courage and daring have been consecrated to the cause of Christ. The course of Christian history might have been changed had not this valiant band remained stanch as a bulwark at the strategic frontier between the Moslem of the Near East and the Moslem of the Far East.

The Turk, out of respect for their valor, and doubtless in deference to the promise of the Prophet, has shown them respect and consideration not vouchsafed to other subject nations. With the Kurds, with whom their nation is commingled, they have maintained perpetual strife.

During the Great War they chose the harder way, and despite the instinctive warning of self-interest, they threw their lot with the Allies. For this they suffer today. Great Britain, conscious of her indebtedness to her smallest ally, has stimulated the complicated machinery of the League of Nations to action in their behalf. The recent decision of the Court of the League does not meet the request of Great Britain or the hope of her ally. It does, however, give some assurance of better living conditions and larger opportunity to the Assyrians. These mountain people will no longer be compelled to live in the plains. Dr. Emhardt, in his

INTRODUCTION

report to the National Council of the Episcopal Church of investigations made by him in 1924, called attention to the decreasing vitality of these people and the devastating infant mortality; and stressed the need of their return to the mountains.

The Episcopal Church has recently sent a priest and a layman as the nucleus of an American unit in the Archbishop of Canterbury's Mission to the Assyrians. This is purely a mission of help to a sister Church, which throughout the centuries has contributed so much in service and martyrdom to maintain the Cross of Christ in this war-swept region.

The writers of this book are qualified to speak. One is an American priest who has followed this ancient Church with loving interest for more than a quarter of a century, and has recently visited the Kingdom of Iraq. The other is a native Assyrian, born in Kurdistan, educated in the English College at Urmia, Persia, and also at our own Theological Seminary of Virginia. He has lived with his people in Europe, and in North and South America.

It is to be hoped that this book will justify the interest of those who know, love, and admire these people in their effort to maintain themselves as a national entity and a Christian communion.

JOHN G. MURRAY,
Presiding Bishop.

THE OLDEST CHRISTIAN PEOPLE

THE OLDEST CHRISTIAN PEOPLE

CHAPTER I

THE REMNANT OF THE ASSYRIANS

AFTER the fall of the Assyrian Empire, overthrown by the power of the allied armies of Persia and Media in 610 B.C., a remnant of the Assyrian race, chiefly composed of princes, noblemen, and warriors, took refuge in the mountains of Kurdistan. Here the Assyrians had previously maintained summer resorts in order to escape the burning sands of Nineveh. To safeguard their interests in this part of the land, they built strong "kalas" or fortresses in which they maintained ample army posts. Some of these fortifications and military barracks still remain. Other traces of Assyrian civilization in these highlands are found in the form of masonry, bricks, bridges, water pipes, spear heads, and many other relics of a native art. Even some of the roads constructed by the Assyrians are still in use in these regions.

Evidently the conquerors of the huge Assyrian Empire were satisfied with their overwhelming victory and the great spoils which they took after the capture of Nineveh, the Assyrian capital, and other wealthy cities in the lower portion of the Empire. The victorious armies were rushing their forces on into Syria and Egypt, which at that time, politically and economically, were within the Assyrian Empire. Therefore, an attempt to conquer the barren regions of Kurdistan would have proved futile, and indeed disastrous to a small invading force. In addition, the Babylonian and Persian armies were recruited from men of the plains who could not traverse these ragged mountain roads, accessible only to a highlander people. If such an expedition had been contemplated therefore by the allied forces, the execution of the plan would probably have been assigned to the Scythians (northern tribesmen). These were mercenary troops more interested in plundering rich cities than in conquering waste lands.

Such were the geographical and strategic conditions which made Kurdistan an asylum and prevented the merciless conquerors from obliterating the Assyrian race. In these lofty mountains the Assyrians remained secluded; there they lived on the memories of past glories and of shattered power, cut off from the rest of their race which had fallen into the hands of their enemies, forgotten and lost forever.

Even the might of Alexander the Great, who penetrated into the heart of the East, and the gallant Roman legions which ruled the East with their strong military organization for so many centuries, made no attempt to conquer these tribes. Trajan, the Roman Emperor, in the second century A.D., marched at the head of the Roman armies through Armenia, touching the northern region of Kurdistan on his way to Persia. Here Roman legionaires fought against the Parthian army. Apparently the Roman generals had made a treaty with the Assyrians similar to that which they made with Armenia, in order to secure a passage for their armies. It is likely that the Assyrian tribes were employed as mercenaries by the Romans. Thus the adopted land of the Assyrians heard the tread of foreign armies, without becoming a field of conflict. On the other hand, the lowlands were a perpetual battlefield for centuries between Roman, Persian, and Parthian emperors who were aspiring to world supremacy. Strains of Roman blood are still found among the southern Assyrians. Among them you can find the blond hair and fair complexion, unknown among the typical Semitic dwellers of the mountainous regions.

The Assyrians of Kurdistan bear a close resemblance to the Hebrews, with their long noses and round-shaped heads. Furthermore, most of the names are similar to those of early Hebrew. Hebrew customs and traditions still prevail. Jewish holidays are strictly observed, and eating pork is strictly prohibited. A kind of animal sacrifice is still practiced. The animal is a family gift to God and is killed at the door of the church. Some of the blood of the victim is smeared on the forehead of the person for whom the animal is sacrificed. The meat is eaten by the priest, the deacon, and the poor. The hide is given to the church. The fat is used for candles. I remember how my mother took me, as a little boy, to one of the ancient shrines. We sacrificed an ox and my mother explained to me that she had promised this gift to God before I was born.

All present-day so-called Assyrians do not seem to be descendants of the ancient race. There is little doubt that the Assyrian tribe, called the Tribe of Jilu, is one of the lost tribes of Israel. This tribe inhabits the eastern part of the district of Hakari. The word Jilu means "captivity" and is derived from the Aramaic word "Gallotha," meaning captivity. It is the richest and one of the strongest of all the Assyrian tribes. Its members are merchants, masons, tradesmen, money lenders, and great travelers in foreign countries. There is a similar type of Assyrian near the Lake of Urmi.

When you pass from Jilu westward into the Tyari and Tikhoma regions, you find the real Assyrian tribe. Both men and women wear long hair and still use the same type of hats worn by the early Assyrians and lately imitated by German military organizations. Their language is a dialectical variant, and their customs to a certain degree are alien to the rest of the Assyrian race. A warlike people, always armed and in constant vigilance, they are reputed the best fighters in the East.

An evidence of the continuity of the Assyrian race is the observance by nearly all of the inhabitants of Kurdistan and lower Assyria of a feast commemorating the journey of the Prophet Jonah to the Assyrian capital. Even the Yezidis, or devil worshippers, and the Kurds regard Jonah as a prophet. In his memory the Assyrians fast three days and nights from food and water and spend most of their time in prayer, offering gifts to God for the salvation of their forefathers, the Ninevites, from the doom predicted by the prophet Jonah.

CHAPTER II

ASSYRIAN TRADITIONS

A CURSORY review of the closing books of the Old Testament will convince any one that the last pages of God's Revelation to His prophets were designed to fit and prepare the Semitic Gentiles for the reception of the Gospels. It is quite natural that the Aramaic-speaking Christians of Nearer Asia should apply to themselves all the references there associated with Nearer Asia. Their traditions enshrine many such events, some of which it is interesting to note.

VISIT OF THE MAGI

Among these treasured traditions is the claim that the Magi who visited the infant Christ were Aramaic-speaking Assyrians. At the time of our Lord the civilized world was under the sway of two great Empires, divided by the Euphrates: the Roman in the west and the Parthian, which superseded the Persian and Grecian dynasties, in the east. Between these still persisted as a semi-autonomous state the smaller kingdom of Urhai or Edessa, which was not considered of sufficient worth to merit the costly conquest of the mountainous regions of a comparatively poor country. In the great commercial world but three languages were current: Greek, Latin, and Aramaic. These were the three languages used by Pilate in the superscription placed upon the cross.

Aramaic, of course, was the form of speech used by the Hebrews in those days.

When the wise men came from the East, therefore, they were supposed to have come from the smaller Aramaic-speaking kingdom of Urhai or Edessa. Tradition asserts that they came in fulfillment of a prophecy made by Zoroaster in the seventh century B.C. It is held that Zoroaster retired from the world at an early age and while sheltered in a lonely cave received a divine vision which unfolded spiritual principles and laws of correct moral life almost equal in beauty to those of the Christian faith. A part of the prophecy put forth by him as a result of these visions was that from the East there should go forth from among his followers Magi or Magians, members of his priestly caste, who under the guidance of a divine light should be led to that great One who was the ruler of the powers of the world. His followers in Aramaic-speaking countries associated this vision with the Messiah, whose coming had been prophesied in their own land during the dispersion and captivity of the Jews. They naturally envisioned him as the divinely chosen Ruler of Israel and spontaneously directed their approach to Jerusalem, inquiring for one who was born King of the Jews.

The Biblical story itself is too well known to need repetition. The Assyrians, however, have other details which they have treasured. They place the number at twelve, in groups of four each, each group bearing an appropriate gift. Thus gold is brought by Arvandid, son of Artiban; Hormsed, son of Satros; Gosnasap, son of Gonapar; and Arshak, son of Mehros. The bearers of myrrh were Zarandar, son of Warzod; Akrehu, son of Kesro; Arbakchest, son of Kolite;

Ashtonkakodon, son of Sheshron. Lastly, frankincense was the gift of Mahros, son of Kohram; Aksherosh, son of Kashan; Sadlak, son of Baldan; and Merodak, son of Bildad.

THE STORY OF KING ABGAR

The Magi, after returning from Bethlehem, are said to have told of the wonderful things they had seen and heard and to have interpreted their significance in such manner as to prepare the Syrian mind for the reception of the Gospel. Within a few years after the Ascension, Christianity was doubtless preached in Mesopotamia and in the Persian Empire. The Jerusalem Talmud testified to a flourishing community in Babylon in 80 A.D. Assyrian tradition claims that St. Peter wrote his first Epistle from the actual city of Babylon and that he tarried in Upper Mesopotamia as he journeyed thither.

The most important traditional event in the preparation of Edessa for the reception of the Gospel is found in a universally accepted tradition of the Eastern Churches of the correspondence between our Lord and King Abgar V (Ukkoma or Uchomo, *the Black*), recorded by the historian Eusebius and in a more extended form in the Syriac Doctrine of Addai (or Thaddeus, said to be one of the Seventy). Both contain a letter from Abgar. Eusebius states that our Lord's reply was verbal, Addai that it was written. It is stated that Abgar, who was a leper, sent an embassy to Eleutheropolis to Sabinus, deputy governor for Tiberius in Phœnicia, Syria, and Mesopotamia. These messengers brought back enthusiastic accounts of the works and preachings of Jesus of Nazareth and of the hostilities of the Jews.

The Doctrine of Addai then quotes the letter of Abgar; which reads as follows:

> From Abgar, the King of Edessa, peace and greetings, to Jesus, the Excellent Saviour, who has appeared on the borders of Judea; I have heard reports concerning thee and thy cures which are performed by thee without medicine and without the use of herbs. It is said that thou causest the blind to see again, the lame to walk, and thou cleanest the lepers, and that thou canst cast out impure spirits and demons. That thou healest those who are tormented by long suffering and thou raisest the dead. And having heard all these things concerning thee, I believe one of two things: Either thou art God, having descended from heaven, and doest these things. Or else doing these you are the Son of God. Therefore, I have written and invited you to visit us and to heal the disease of which I am suffering. I have also heard that the Jews are against thee and are seeking to harm thee. I have a rather small but noble city which is sufficient for both of us.

JESUS' REPLY TO ABGAR

> Blessed art thou, O Abgar, who without seeing hast believed in me. For it is written about me that they who had seen me will not believe, and they who had not seen me may believe and live. But in regard to what thou hast written, that I shall come to thee. It is necessary that I fulfill all

things here for which I have been sent, and
then to be received again by Him that sent
me. And after I have been received up I
will send thee one of my disciples that he
may heal thy disease and give life to thee
and those who are with thee.

Whatever the antiquity and historical value
of these statements, we must not forget that they
form part of the traditions of an ancient Church,
noted for its missionary zeal and fidelity to the
faith under direst persecutions. It is important
to note that Eleutheropolis was given that name
by Septimus Severus about 200 A. D. This corresponds with the date of the visit of King Abgar
IX, who either was actually converted to
Christianity or showed a most favorable attitude
toward Christians in general.

HANAN'S PORTRAIT OF CHRIST

After quoting this letter of Jesus, the doctrine
of Addai goes on to state:

But when Hanan the Archivist perceived
that Jesus thus spoke to him, he, because he
was the painter of the kings, painted a picture of Jesus with chosen colors and brought
it to King Abgar, his master. When King
Abgar saw the picture he accepted it with
great delight and gave it a place of honor
in one of his palaces.

The historian Hume considers this picture
worthy of special note. Of course, his treatment
of the subject is satirical; but he recognizes the
important place it held in the life of the Church,
not only in the East, but also in the West. It
was evidently guarded carefully for centuries;
and recourse was had to its protective power

during the siege of Edessa by Chosroes Nushviran. Its exposure upon the ramparts of the city led to the confusion and dispersion of the Persian host. Toward the end of the sixth century it was copied, and these copies became objects of veneration. When Edessa finally succumbed to Moslem assaults, the picture was seized by the conquerors. After three hundred years it was handed over to Constantinople: "For a ransom of twelve pounds of silver, for the redemption of two hundred Mussulmans, and a perpetual truce for the territory of Edessa." Later it fell into the hands of the Franciscans and all trace of it was lost.

SAINT THOMAS

Several early traditions of the East center around Saint Thomas. Saint John's translation of his Aramaic name by its Greek equivalent Didymus or twin gave rise to many Gnostic speculations which identified his cult with one resembling that of the Heavenly Twins, Castor and Pollux. This is especially shown in the ancient Syriac *Acta Thomæ*, where he seems to be considered as the twin brother of our Lord Himself. Their acts and revelations are closely interwoven. Other traditions consider him the twin of a sister Lysias, and his birthplace, Antioch.

Earliest traditions associate him with Edessa, to which place he sent Addai or Theaddaeus, whom we have mentioned before. Thither, all Eastern traditions claim, his bones were sent. Traditions of about the fourth century send him to India, where he suffered martyrdom. Even these Indian traditions link him with Parthia.

The one recognized historical personage in *Acta Thomæ*, which tells of the founding of the Indian Church, is Gundaphar, who undoubtedly is the Parthian Gondophares, whose sovereignty extended into India. Critical analysis of the *Acta* shows that both in topography and nomenclature they reveal a Syriac pen.

The *Acta Thomæ* is by far the most interesting piece of Syriac literature, both in itself and because of a remarkable poem called *The Hymn of the Soul* which it contains. The story relates how, after the Ascension, the apostles divide among themselves the several spheres of influence and missionary endeavor. India is assigned to Thomas, who is called Judas Thomas, or Judas the Twin. Thomas objects and our Lord appears in a dream to Habban, the servant of Gundaphar, King of India, and sells Thomas to him as a slave. After many adventures and numerous miracles, healings, resurrections, and casting out of devils, Thomas arrives in India. Unlike the other apostles, he preaches a doctrine of individual salvation, with no regard to a Catholic Church. Personal austerity, perpetual virginity, and surrender of self to a happy contemplation of death as the doorway to eternal bliss, are the burden of his message. He seems unconscious of the challenge of Christianity in the surrounding idolatry, and of the necessity of controverting the contentions of the Jews. His fame grows, and his converts are abundant. Success seems to have crowned his efforts until his activities penetrated to the royal household. He is then imprisoned and put to death by four spearmen; and thus is he represented in early Christian art. Before death he ordains Wizan, the king's son. Later, dust from the grave of

Thomas drives away a devil from one of the king's sons. The king is converted and pleads forgiveness.

Thus ends one of the most remarkable apocryphal writings of the Christian Church. Toward the end of the story, St. Thomas, while in prison, sings a Hymn called *The Hymn of the Soul*, so unique that it deserves to be repeated in full.

THE HYMN OF THE SOUL

I

While I was yet but a little child in the House of my Father,
Brought up in luxury, well content with the life of the Palace,
Far from the East, our home, my parents sent me to travel,
And from the royal Hoard they prepared me a load for the journey,
Precious it was, yet light, that alone I carried the burden.

II

Median gold it contained and silver from Atropatene,
Garnet and ruby from Hindostan and Bactrian agate,
Adamant harness was girded upon me stronger than iron;
But my Robe they took off wherewith their love had adorned me,
And the Bright Tunic woven of scarlet and wrought to my stature.

III

For they decreed, and wrote on my heart that I should not forget it;

ASSYRIAN TRADITIONS

"If thou go down and bring from Egypt the Pearl, the unique one,
"Guarded there in the Sea that envelopes the loud-hissing Serpent,
"Thou shalt be clothed again with thy Robe and the Tunic of Scarlet,
"And with thy Brother, the Prince, shalt thou inherit the Kingdom."

IV

So I quitted the East, two Guardians guiding me downwards,
Hard was the way for a child and a dangerous journey to travel,
Soon I had passed Maishan, the mart of the Eastern merchants,
Over the soil of Babylon then I hurried my footsteps,
And my companions left me within the borders of Egypt.

V

Straight to the Serpent I went and near him settled my dwelling,
Till he should slumber and sleep, and the Pearl I could snatch from his keeping,
I was alone, an exile under a foreign dominion,
None did I see of the free-born of the Easterns,
Save one youth, a son of Maishan, who became my companion.

VI

He was my friend to whom I told the tale of my venture,
Warned him against the Egyptians and all their ways of uncleanness;

Yet in their dress I clothed myself to escape recognition,
Being afraid lest when they saw that I was a stranger
Come from afar for the Pearl, they would rouse the Serpent against me.

VII

It was from him perchance they learnt I was none of their kindred,
And in their guile they gave me to eat of their unclean dainties;
Thus I forgot my race and I served the King of the country,
Nay, I forgot the Pearl for which my parents had sent me,
While from their poisonous food I sank into unconscious slumber.

VIII

All that had chanced my Parents knew and they grieved for me sorely,
Through the land they proclaimed for all at our Gate to assemble—
Parthian Princes and Kings, and all the Eastern Chieftains—
There they devised an escape that I should not perish in Egypt,
Writing a letter signed in the name of each of the Chieftains.

IX

"From thy Father, the King of Kings,—From the Queen, thy mother,—
"And from the Brother,—to thee, our Son in Egypt, be greeting!

ASSYRIAN TRADITIONS

"Up and arise from sleep, and hear the words of our letter!

"Thou art a son of Kings; by whom art thou held in bondage?

"Think of the Pearl for which thou wast sent to sojourn in Egypt.

X

"Think of thy shining Robe and remember thy glorious Tunic;

"These thou shalt wear when thy name is enrolled in the list of the heroes,

"And with thy Brother Viceroy thou shalt be in the Kingdom,"

This was my letter, sealed with the King's own seal on the cover,

Lest it should fall in hands of the fierce Babylonian demons.

XI

High it flew as the Eagle, King of the birds of the heaven,

Flew and alighted beside me, and spoke in the speech of my country,

Then at the sound of its tones I started and rose from my slumber;

Taking it up I kissed and broke the Seal that was on it,

And like the words engraved on my heart were the words of the letter.

XII

So I remembered my Royal race and my free-born nature,

So I remembered the Pearl, for which they had sent me to Egypt,
And I began to charm the terrible loud-hissing Serpent:
Down he sank into sleep at the sound of the Name of my Father,
And at my Brother's Name, and the Name of the Queen, my Mother.

XIII

Then I seized the Pearl and homewards started to journey,
Leaving the unclean garb I had worn in Egypt behind me;
Straight for the East I set my course, to light of the homeland,
And on the way in front I found the Letter that roused me—
Once it awakened me, now it became a Light to my pathway.

XIV

For with its silken folds it shone on the road I must travel,
And with its voice and leading cheered my hurrying footsteps,
Drawing me on in love across the perilous passage,
Till I had left the land of Babylon safely behind me
And I had reached Maishan, the sea-washed haven of merchants.

XV

What I had worn of old, my Robe with its Tunic of Scarlet,

Thither my Parents sent from the far Hycranian mountains,
Brought by the hand of the faithful warders who had it in keeping;
I was a child when I left it nor could its fashion remember,
But when I looked, the Robe had received my form and likeness.

XVI

It was myself that I saw before me as in a mirror;
Two in number we stood, yet only one in appearance,
Not less alike than the strange twin guardian figures
Bringing my Robe, each marked with the Royal Escutcheon,
Servants both of the King whose troth restored me my Treasure.

XVII

Truly a royal Treasure appeared my Robe in its glory,
Gay it shone with beryl and gold, sardonyx and ruby,
Over its varied hues there flashed the colour of sapphire,
All its seams with stones of adamant firmly were fastened,
And upon all the King of Kings Himself was depicted.

XVIII

While I gazed it sprang into life as a sentient creature,
Even as if endowed with speech and hearing I saw it,

When I heard the tones of its voice as it cried to the keepers;
"He, the Champion, he for whom I was reared by the Father—
"Hast thou not marked me, how my stature grew with his labours?"

XIX

All the while with a kingly mien my Robe was advancing,
Flowing towards me as if impatient with those who bore it;
I, too, longed for it, ran to it, grasped it, put it upon me,
Once again I was clothed in my Robe and adorned with its beauty,
And the bright many-hued Tunic again was gathered about me.

XX

Clad in the Robe I betook me up to the Gate of the Palace,
Bowing my head to the glorious Sign of my Father that sent it;
I had performed His behest and He had fulfilled what He promised,
So in the Satraps' Court I joined the throng of the Chieftains—
He with favour received me and near Him I dwell in the Kingdom.[1]

[1] Translation by F. Crawford Burkitt.

CHAPTER III

THE EVANGELIZATION OF THE ASSYRIANS

THE Assyrian Church claims to be the first organized Christian community in the world. Apostolic customs and traditions are still preserved. Its liturgical books and its teachings are still in Aramaic, the language which Christ spoke and in which the earliest Christian documents were written. These Assyrians are the only pure Semites within the fold of the Christian Church.

At the time when Christianity first was preached to the Assyrians, the Eastern religions were gradually losing their strength. Seeds of Western culture had been sown during the Greek and Roman conquests, and results were apparent in many countries which had come within the sphere of these influences. The mystic cults of the East were losing their hold on the intellectual and higher classes. Free thinking resulted from the study of Greek philosophy and logic. Changes of front in the old faith were frequent in Eastern countries. Zoroastrianism was weakening and merging into a new form of faith, later known as Mithraism.

This religion of Mithra was one of the most refined of the Eastern cults and, ethically, close to Christianity. Mithraism was the religion of the army, and so did not appeal to the hearts of the masses who were rapidly becoming enslaved by the power of Rome and Oriental monarchs.

Mithra, the divinity of this sect, was supposed to have been born from a rock. Its doctrines and dogmas are extremely magical and allegorical in form and content.

Most Eastern cults at the time of the advent of Christianity literally had become corrupted and reduced to mockery, because of the practice of magic and priestly witchcraft. Religion was largely in the hands of soothsayers and fortune tellers, who preyed on the credulity of the public and the name of gods and demons.

Undoubtedly a great part of the success of the Christian religion in the East can be attributed to the facility of approach which it possessed through similarity of customs and manners. The absence of these natural points of contact made the progress of early Christianity more difficult in the West. Christianity is an Eastern religion, revealed through Eastern thinkers, and in the garb of Eastern customs. Indeed, all Eastern religions, whether good or bad, served as contributory sources to the spread of the religion of the Hebrews, and later of Christianity. The religion of Christ was the consummation of the hope of Judaism. Christ unveiled the Hebrew mysteries, and the Hebraic religious concept was brought to fruition and universality. Hitherto, Hebrews, as well as other Eastern people, were enslaved in spirit through religion. They thought of a man as a slave to God, and of obedience to the law as his only means of salvation. Christ was the first prophet to proclaim that man was not created for the uses of religion, but religion for the uses of man. Therefore, religious tidings carrying this inspiring message and bearing this new character penetrated the hearts of Eastern worshippers. The Fatherhood

EVANGELIZATION OF ASSYRIANS

of God and the brotherhood of man were for the first time proclaimed to men wearied by a religion of bondage. This proclamation appealed to the downtrodden classes in the East, who were eager to revolt and free themselves from the tyranny of priests and the feudalistic rulers upheld by them.

We must remember that the apostles were Orientals of the Semitic type. They went to neighboring communities and preached to people who were racial kinsmen and whose social customs and traditions offered natural points of contact. Furthermore, at this time nearly all Syrians, including the Assyrians, used the Aramaic language, and could readily understand the words in which "Good Tidings" were first proclaimed.

In the West, Christianity had to face many natural difficulties growing out of the proneness of the Greek mind to philosophic analysis, and the jealousy felt by the Romans to any claim that did not conform to their program of imperialism or lend itself to legalistic codification. A suffering Messiah was a stumbling block to the Greek; and a triumphant malefactor a contradiction to the Roman. In the East, even the natural religions were "school masters" to bring us to Christ. Mithraism taught of a God who triumphed over evil and ascended to the heavens. Even Assyria and Babylon had made their contributions toward the opening of the Kingdom of Heaven to true believers. The Babylonians worshipped Marduk, who had been put to death unjustly and raised in victory. The idea of supernatural birth was acceptable to nearly all the cults of Mesopotamia.

Material circumstances, too, favored the ready conversion of the East. Commercial relations between the Empire and the East were excellent. Never before was the world blessed with such peace and tranquillity. Merchants and travelers went freely to the East, seeking commercial opportunities. National and racial antipathies were fading and gradually giving way before the fruits of commercial prosperity which the Empire was offering to its subjects.

At the same time, the picture continually mirrored in the ambitious minds of the Roman Emperors was the consolidation and the unification of the complex races of the East, and the problem of remoulding them into a united empire. Thus the policy of the state tended to discourage religious antagonisms within subject nations.

While Christianity was spreading under conditions favorable to the integrity of the faith in the East, trials befell the Church in the West which led to suffering, confusion, and discord.

Persecutions for a time strengthened the faith of the believers and largely contributed to the rapid spread of Christianity in the West. The blood of the martyrs was the seed that grew so rapidly and in the end so signally triumphed over imperial Rome. Nevertheless, at just this time these persecutions were not only a menace to the little loyal army of Christ, but a real catastrophe to Christian literature. The people had just begun to appreciate the faith of Christ and His sacrifices for humanity. The Gospels were not yet written, and most men who possessed valuable information concerning the life of Christ suffered at the hands of the enemy. The whole group of the Faithful was disorganized and literary activities rendered almost impossible.

If the persecutions had not started so soon in the Roman Empire, Christianity would have been prepared more fully to meet controversies, and today we probably would have had additional early documentary statements concerning Christ and His Teachings.

It was not so in the Persian Empire. There Christianity was tolerated. There the Church won into its fold men and women of noble families, who in many cases gained special favors for it from the king and governmental authorities. At this period the Persian religion was disorganized, and the Magi, the "fire worshippers," could offer little resistance to the aggressive power of Christianity.

For nearly three hundred years persecutions were unknown. The Church was progressing so rapidly that missionary centers had been established in various neighboring countries. Institutions of learning were created, and the Church gave birth to literary scholars, such as Bardazen, Tatian, and Ephrem the Great.

Study of Eastern diplomacy will readily show that the Persian government at this time looked on Christianity as a religion which had its source in the Roman Empire, promulgated by a group of Roman citizens who were constantly protesting and condemning the Roman government for its extreme penalty to One whom they worshipped as their God and King. Patriotic Persians saw in this movement a military and revolutionary opportunity. Roman persecutions of Christians were becoming intense and, in consequence, were weakening the Empire. Persians saw in Christianity a new movement which was altering the old Roman system, Roman organization, and the course of Roman history, by reducing the Roman Emperor from a god to a worshipper of One whom his predecessors had condemned and crucified as a malefactor.

The constant stream of Christian refugees into Persia offered ground enough to make the Persian authorities sympathetic toward those they viewed as "enemies of Rome." They thought that, in the event of hostilities between these two great powers, the Christians would naturally enlist their forces on the side of the Persian government. This expectation never was realized. The hidden Christian leaven finally leavened the whole Roman Empire with its ferment, and the Emperor became chief in command of the Faithful. Then the Persian policy toward Christianity suddenly changed. It was now plain that the Roman Empire had just emerged from a dying Paganism into a new religion of zeal and power, a religion promoting such strong convictions that its adherents were willing to die for the cause. The Persian government proclaimed Christianity a hostile movement and proceeded to drive this dangerous element from its confines.

With friendly relations impaired between Christianity and the Persian government, the Sun Worshippers regained favor in the eyes of the king and court. They combatted Christianity by philosophical argument and logic. They tried to prove to the Persian King of Kings that Christianity was nothing but a mockery. Indeed, it was almost unthinkable that Christ should aspire to be acknowledged the superior of their Sun God Mazda! Christ, a man, born and reared in Judea and finally killed by enemies who had plotted against him; a man whose growth was due to the joyful light and heat of the Sun and one who had eaten food which was produced by its golden rays!

EVANGELIZATION OF ASSYRIANS

Thus ended the three hundred years of peace in the East. Efforts made by the Emperor Constantine to establish better relations between Eastern Christians and the Persian government were discontinued at his death.

While the Church in the Roman Empire emerged from an era of persecution, the Eastern Christians entered into a season of bloody testimony, far sharper in its intensity than that from which the Western Christians had suffered for three hundred years, which finally disrupted the Church and made possible the subjugation of the Christian Church in the East by the power of Islam.

CHAPTER IV

ROMAN AND PERSIAN WARS

LEAVING Church activities for a while, let us examine the political and economic relations at this time between the East and the West.

Even though several minor conflicts occurred in the first century B. C., between the Romans and the Parthians, the first century A. D. passed peaceably. Real conflict arose over Armenia, which generally was a natural ally of the Parthians, their racial kin. However, when the Parthians tried unjustly to annex this small ally, she appealed for help to Rome.

In the year 114 A. D., Trajan marched at the head of the Roman army toward the East, and his forces passed through Armenia. Finally he was defeated at Hatra, an Assyrian town near the river Tigris. The Parthians took a large number of prisoners, among them many Christians.

In 150 A. D., Cassius, a Roman general, defeated the Parthian army and burned Seleucia, a Persian city of nearly five hundred thousand inhabitants. On the other hand, the Parthians won several decisive victories over the Romans, but they could not create a stable government in Persia.

In 216 A. D., Ardashir, son of Babak, ended the Parthian rule, and established the Sassinide Dynasty. This was the strongest Persian government in the East during the period between the establishment of Christianity and the advent of Islam. Some kings of this dynasty were severe and others were very tolerant toward Christianity.

After the death of Ardassir, the founder of the dynasty, his son Sapor ascended the throne of a well-organized empire (240-273 A.D.). In the year 260 A. D., Valerian, the Roman Emperor, declared war, promising to avenge the Roman blood that had been shed and to destroy Persia. Roman gods did not favor these adventurous expeditions. The emperor was taken captive and the entire Roman army destroyed. Hundreds of thousands of captives were taken and much booty. Meanwhile, Sapor penetrated into Syria, destroying, burning, and captives seized in large numbers. These Christian captives were welcomed and cared for by the Christians in Persia, who generously responded to the physical and spiritual needs of their brethren, supplying them with ministers and churches.

In 277 A. D., Carus, a Roman emperor, led the Roman legions once more into Persia, conquering, destroying, and inflicting heavy losses. He was determined to lay waste the whole country, even cutting down the trees. When the emperor, who was bald-headed, received ambassadors sent by the Persian king to seek a conditional armistice, he took off his hat and showed them his bald head, saying, "Go and tell your master that there will be no peace until I make the whole of Persia as bare as my head." The emperor was killed by lightning, and the Roman dreams ended in disaster.

Sapor II ascended the Persian throne 310 A. D. He was elected to the crown before he was born, his father having died without other issue before his birth. During the time of his youth relations with Rome were excellent. A treaty for fifty years of peace was signed between Constantine and the Persian government, which remained effective until the death of Constantine, 337 A. D. Constantine was aware that an Empire which had just emerged from revolutions could not carry further campaigns into the East. After the death of Constantine, Constantius, his son, who succeeded him in the East, did not follow the policy of his father. Sapor II started severe persecutions against the Christians. Both governments were growing impatient and massing forces in the Assyrian lowlands. Before hostilities began Constantius died, leaving his throne to his cousin Julian. In 350, Sapor II declared war and Julian proceeded with a large Roman force toward the East. He tried to follow the same military route as Trajan, thus carrying his Roman troops through Armenia. The Armenians this time sided with Persia and refused passage to the Roman forces. Julian, therefore, was forced to attack the Persian capital. He brought his army to Nesibin in Assyria. The Roman army was defeated and the brave Emperor died at Samara, a little Assyrian town on the Tigris. His successor, eager for peace and hoping to save the Roman army from catastrophe, was willing to cede five rich Roman provinces in Assyria to Persia. This was one of the greatest losses which Rome had ever suffered in her Eastern conflicts. The terms of the treaty included a clause for the evacuation of these provinces by Roman citizens. Many Christians were taken as captives to the interior of Persia. The Assyrian School of Theology at Nesibin was closed and a new school established at Edessa, near the river Khebor. Here Mar Ephraim founded a famous school of the-

ROMAN AND PERSIAN WARS

ology, medicine, and allied sciences. Later Edessa became known as the second Athens.

The news of the Roman defeat was received with much dismay and anxiety by the Christians in the East. They lost hope of release from the Persian yoke. The Persian government celebrated the victory with Oriental pomp. The Assyrian Patriarch at Seleucia, Mar Shimon Bar Sabaye, was summoned by the King to answer various charges brought against him by the Pagan priests. The Patriarch was a close friend of the King and the latter made every possible effort to save him. The demand was made that the Patriarch and the Christian people bow to the Sun as a symbol of their loyalty to the Persian government and the Persian religion. Nothing could shake the faith of the Patriarch, and after days of imprisonment and torture he was executed with hundreds of his clergy. Persecution became more intense as the Magis kept pressing new charges. Sapor II died after a long reign of seventy years, but the Persian policy of persecution continued.

While these events were taking place in Persia, the Christians in the West were experiencing new difficulties. The missionary zeal, stimulated formerly by persecution, had relaxed, and the Church was becoming a department of the State. The Church showed the vices of prosperity and the clergy bore the fruit of idleness. The Church became involved in doctrinal controversies which could not but prove disastrous to an organization just emerging from three hundred years of persecution. In the East, on the other hand, the preservation of the Church itself absorbed all its mental and physical energies.

It is astonishing how little Eastern Christians

knew of the development and theological disputes in the Roman Empire. The Assyrian Church at this time was independent and isolated. Communication with Antioch was cut off. The Council of Seleucia, 410 A. D., declared that the supreme head was the Catholicos of Seleucia, because the West was inaccessible. The Nicene Creed, when brought to the attention of the Eastern divines, was accepted, but later diverging interest and philological misunderstanding created a breach in the unity of the Church.

CHAPTER V

NESTORIUS AND THE ASSYRIANS

It cannot be asserted with justice to historical fact that Nestorius was the founder of the Assyrian Church. The term Nestorians is a "nickname" given to this Christian community which had been in existence four hundred years before Nestorius was born.

Nestorius was a Greek, born and reared in the Byzantine Empire, educated at Antioch, and created Patriarch of Constantinople. Neither before his ordination nor during his great ecclesiastical career had he visited the East. The Assyrians became known as Nestorians, because of their hospitality and the Christian service which they rendered to the Christian refugees to Persia who were condemned as heretics and banished from the Roman Empire.

As we have said in the previous chapter, at the time when Western Christianity was aflame with diverse doctrinal controversies, the Christians in the East were enduring great persecution. Most of the Eastern Bishops had fled and taken refuge in mountains and caves. Christian communities had been disbanded. Consequently, circumstances did not allow the Eastern Bishops to indulge in religious disputes.

So ruthless was the warfare against the Christians in the East that any favorable remark or friendly manifestation toward fellow Christians in the Roman Empire was looked upon as treasonable by the Persian authorities. Those who indulged in such conversations were indicted as conspirators and condemned to capital punishment. The sole task of the Eastern Bishops at that time was the saving of the Church. They had no time to take sides in Western controversies.

Nestorius, a graduate from the Theological School of Antioch, was selected by the Emperor Theodosius for the Patriarchate of Constantinople. He was a great scholar, lecturer, and an eloquent speaker. The Imperial Capital was eager to get a man of such distinction to preside over congregations which were growing fashionable in the religious home of government officials. In the year 428 A. D., he was consecrated Patriarch of Constantinople and highly honored by the Emperor and residents of the Imperial City.

After his consecration and accession to this office, his prime desire was to stamp out Arianism. Like Athanasius he aimed to be a great defender of the faith and the arch enemy of those who sought to detract from the Person of Christ. In the course of his battle against the Arians he confronted a new heresy, that of Apollinaris. The Arians were not only contending that the flesh was the human side of Christ, but were reducing his Deity to one of lesser degree than that of his Father. They said that the Son was created by the Father. The Apollinarians, who were condemning this heresy, in stressing the deity of Christ, minimized His humanity. Nestorius brought about a new crisis through his treatment of these two theological aspects of the controversy. In his preaching he attacked the teaching of Cyril, Bishop of Alexandria. He argued that Mary is not "theotokos," Mother of

NESTORIUS AND THE ASSYRIANS 51

God, but that she was the Mother of Christ; that the Second Person of the Trinity was not born of the Virgin; that Christ died on the Cross, as a man; that His deity did not suffer on the cross. "How can Mary give birth to God who is her creator?" "If God died who can raise Him from the dead?" Such were the strong Nestorian arguments against the Alexandrian doctrines. In turn, he endeavored to prove that Christ lived on earth as a perfect man and as perfect God. He thought that the doctrines of Cyril weakened the humanity of Christ in ways that ought not to be granted.

Nestorius encountered his greatest difficulties when he tried to define the nature of the person of Christ for himself. He used the supplementary Aramaic term of "konoma," a variant for "person" which cannot adequately be translated into a Western language, stating that Christ had two natures, one person and two "konomas." Eventually he could not explain the dual personality in Christ, and was not able to define the word "konoma" sharply enough.

There is no doubt that the basic principles of Nestorius' teachings were taken from the works of Diodore of Tarsus and Theodore of Mopsuestia. Both were great theologians and teachers in the school of Antioch, which openly opposed the allegorical and theoretical teachings of Alexandria. Consequently, such statements as "Mary is the Mother of God" were too confusing for acceptance by the Antiochian theologians who followed the Syrian tradition. Such utterances, when translated into Syriac, define the Person of Christ weakly. The Syriac word for Son is "Bar," derived from the word "BARA," meaning to create. When, therefore, God was said to be the son of Mary, the Christian doctrine of the deity appeared to be reduced to the level of a mere form of Paganism. Nestorius said, "I cannot speak of a God being two or three months old." In his letter to Pope Celestine, Bishop of Rome, he said, "If the Godhead of the Son had its origin in the womb of the Virgin, then it was not a Godhead like that of the Father, and He who was born could not be homoousios with the Father, which was just what the Arians denied Him to be." They said that if God was born, then there was a time when He did not exist.

The intellectual atmosphere was different in Alexandria, for these people had just emerged from Paganism and still cherished live traditions concerning Egyptian gods who had been born, grown old, and died. All around them in their city were the relics of Pagan religion, images of gods who had wives, concubines, sons, and daughters. Here and there stood effigies of the Goddess Isis with a child in her arms. Hence the theological discussions of the Alexandrians did not sound foreign but were in line with inherited thought, and in harmony with general public sentiment. Unfortunately, the debate between Cyril and Nestorius became so bitter and was conducted in such a heat that neither side had the opportunity to explain its terms or position soberly.

The real issue in the struggle was no question of the Person of Christ, but one of rivalry between the sees of Antioch and Alexandria. In its final phase this controversy developed into a clash between Semitic thought and Greek philosophy. It was impossible for men of Semitic training to encompass the subtleties of thought which were current in Greece and Alexandria.

The distinctions and the technical terms used could not be translated nor explained in Semitic language.

While Nestorius defended the humanity of Christ, he was to some degree supporting Apollinarianism. Cyril, in defending the Divinity, seemed to him to be defending the views of Arius, who just a century before had been condemned because he had said that the Second Person was not equal to the Father.

At the outset the Bishop of Rome took no real interest in the controversy. He depended for his facts upon the letters Cyril wrote to him, at a time when the friendly relations between Celestine and Nestorius were partially broken, because Nestorius had given asylum to Pelagian priests who had been banished by Western Bishops.

THE COUNCIL OF EPHESUS

The tension between these opposing parties became so great that it shook the very foundations of the Church throughout the Christian empire. Deliberate efforts made by the Emperor and Bishops to settle the dispute were in vain. When the Emperor saw that the temper of the disputants was constantly growing more hostile and menacing to the peace of the Empire, he summoned all the Patriarchs with their Bishops to Ephesus for a Council. He decided to have a government representative preside at the meeting and appointed Candadian as Imperial Commissioner. Before the Patriarch of Antioch and other Eastern Bishops could arrive, the Western Bishops, aware that Theodosius had been lenient toward Nestorius, grew restive. Despite strong protests on the part of Candadian and those who were sympathizers with Nestorius, they opened the Council and abruptly condemned Nestorius and his teachings. Nestorius refused to appear before the Synod on the ground that the entire body present consisted of his open enemies, and that the Eastern Bishops had not yet arrived. Soon after the Council adjourned the Eastern Bishops arrived, headed by John, Patriarch of Antioch, who became very angry and called his party together in a council in the same city which condemned Cyril and the work of the preceding council. The Patriarch of Antioch, supported by Candadian, tried to depose both Cyril and the Bishop of Ephesus. At the same time the Emperor issued a manifesto declaring the sessions of the first Council invalid, on the ground that Nestorius had been anathematized unheard, and that Cyril's party had ignored the orders of the Imperial representative. Later he confirmed the depositions pronounced on both sides, thus placing Cyril and Nestorius under arrest.

THE COUNCIL OF CHALCEDON

Regardless of the Imperial edict against Cyril and Nestorius and their teachings, the fire still kept burning. Both parties were active in advocating their positions. The Emperor, tired of dissension and eager for peace, called another council at Chalcedon, at which the majority of the Bishops supported Cyril and condemned Nestorius. The Emperor reluctantly yielded to the majority, when he saw that even John, Patriarch of Antioch, had deserted his friend Nestorius and had made peace with Cyril, thus reversing himself. He was now willing to suppress what he

NESTORIUS AND THE ASSYRIANS

had supported previously and to condemn the theology of Antioch. Nestorius was deprived of his high office and banished first to Antioch and then to a desert in Egypt, where he died in exile. Meanwhile, those who adhered to the teachings of Nestorius were persecuted and also banished. Some of them went to Arabia, but most of his followers took refuge in Assyria and Persia.

Other Antiochian teachers who followed Nestorius went to Nesibin. Because they were Roman refugees, the Persian government again manifested a tolerant spirit toward them. At this time, Bar Suma and Ibas of Edessa, both supporters of the Antiochian theology and friends of Nestorius, were at Nesibin. As an advisor of the Persian King, and with the King's support, Bar Suma issued a proclamation compelling all Eastern Bishops to accept the teachings of Nestorius without reservations. The news was received with calmness on the part of the Eastern Bishops, and very little resistance was made to the decree. Events were now more favorable to the Christians in Persia who hitherto had endured stormy persecutions.

The Eastern Bishops rejected the Council of Chalcedon on the following grounds:

1. That the Council was not ecumenical because hundreds of Bishops did not arrive in time to participate in its decisions.

2. That Nestorius was unjustly condemned by a group of his enemies.

3. That the doctrine introduced by Cyril, that Mary was the Mother of God, was not to be found either in the Gospels or in the teachings of the Early Fathers. Meanwhile, in the East, Mary was called the Mother of the Lord.

Throughout the theological controversies which were taking place in the Roman Empire, the Eastern Christians had always maintained their orthodox faith concerning the natures and the person of Christ. The following is an extract from the Assyrian prayer book:

> One is Jesus, Son of God, worshipped by all in His two natures. In His divinity begotten of the Father without beginning before time. In His humanity born of Mary in the fullness of time, in organic body. His divinity is not from the essence of the mother, and His humanity is not from the essence of the Father. The natures are kept in their "konomas"[1] (Epostasion) in one person and one sonship. Just as there are three Persons in one Deity; such is the sonship of the son, two natures, one person.

Such was the crisis which split Christendom. Such were the teachings and doctrines which widened the breach between East and West and inflicted those deep wounds which ultimately caused the decline of Christianity in the East.

[1] The Greek Epostasion is the nearest equivalent of the Syriac 'konoma.'

CHAPTER VI

NESTORIAN CUSTOMS AND PRACTICES

THE development of the Church of the East has been traced until it had reached its period of expansion. Its doctrine, discipline, and practices were fixed. The East never changes. Hence we find these identical customs and practices continued to this day. Some of them it will be profitable to note.

THE PRIESTHOOD

The Assyrians, as has been said, are of the purest Semitic type and therefore are racially related to the Hebrews, with whom they have many common customs and traditions. The present Assyrian priesthood is similar to that of the old Aaronic priestly order. This is divided into three major divisions—deacons, priests, and bishops, and each division is divided into three subdivisions, as follows:
- (1) bishops, metropolitans, and patriarchs
- (2) priests, archdeacons, and *chor sposkopos* (suffragan bishops)
- (3) church care-takers, sub-deacons, and deacons.

Generally the Assyrian priesthood is hereditary. Some of them come from old families whose vocation has always been religion and whose interests are devoted to maintaining tribal morality.

58 THE OLDEST CHRISTIAN PEOPLE

The Patriarch is not only the ecclesiastical head, but also the temporal ruler. The Patriarch is always a Nazarite. From his childhood he must abstain from eating meat, or shaving his beard. He must not marry. From youth he is instructed concerning his high office and his duty as a representative of Christ on earth. While "growing in wisdom and stature," he already realizes that he has given himself to God. His people consider him as the representative man of their race. His entire life is spent in fasting and prayer. His functions are temporal as well as spiritual. The Patriarch's chief duties in spiritual matters are to ordain the archbishops and bishops, and occasionally other clergy. He lays hands on the sick and forgives the sins of his people in the name of Christ. He appoints maliks (tribal chiefs) and looks after the political welfare of his people. He is the chief religious, financial, and legal advisor in all tribal matters. He is succeeded by his nephew or oldest unmarried brother.

The metropolitan and bishop are also Nazarites and exercise the same functions as the Patriarch in their own dioceses under the guidance of the Patriarch. Most of them are self-sacrificing. They live in modest houses, fasting and praying. When the poor come to their door they share with them all their meager supplies. They are maintained by free will offerings taken at certain shrines. At times they exercise the gift of healing.

The Assyrian priest has more freedom. He can eat meat and can marry. When his wife dies he is allowed to marry again. His office is one of extreme importance and delicacy, as he has to deal directly with the uneducated and illiterate masses. These priests are clerics, tax collectors, mayors, merchants, healers, and agriculturalists. They conduct morning service at three o'clock and then follow their daily routine. The priests are supported by a share of the harvest set aside for them, by gifts, and marriage and baptismal fees. The parishioners generally give twenty per cent of all their agricultural produce to the priest, and every male person works a day annually for him. They also receive a part of the gifts brought to the shrines by the worshippers.

The training of the Assyrian priest is confined to a study of the Psalms of David and other liturgical books, morning prayer and the breviary. The priest can read all of the Scriptures, and he has to repeat from memory the prayers and the mass. As we have said in the previous chapters, the Assyrian Church has lost its institutions and theological schools. Since the advent of the Mongols and their conquest of the East, the Church has not produced any men of literary preëminence.

The priest reads the service in Syriac in the church, and after his reading of the gospel he preaches. The sermons are not of an expository character; nor does the priest attempt to interpret the Scriptures. His discourse is most simple and practical. As a rule, the priest preaches the same sermon throughout his whole ministry. It contains warnings against those who are guilty of breaking moral laws, or are guilty of crime, and against those who do not fast and pray. All pronouncements made by the priests are accepted by the people as of divine inspiration.

During the conflicts with the Kurds, the Priests marched at the head of the Assyrian army, just as did the priests of Levitical times. They also take part in most of the public festivals, and other social activities. Invariably the entire community looks to them for spiritual and temporal leadership and advice.

THE CHURCH

The Assyrian Church is noted for her ancient temples. Some of these old buildings date from the second and third centuries A. D. Excepting a portion of the door which is made of wood, the entire structure is of solid stone and of an architecture highly developed. The walls are ten feet thick; the buildings are very dark for they have only a very few small windows, about two feet by three. These Assyrian churches are destitute of all relics. There are no statues nor images, save the Cross, for which the Assyrians feel a great veneration. The temple is divided into different chapels just as was the temple of Solomon. There is a chapel for daily prayer, another for burial, one for baptism, and still another for marriage. But the important part of the church is the "kanki"—the holy of holies, which is separated from the rest of the temple by a wall. No one can enter this sanctuary except priests and deacons, and they only providing they are fasting. Only on Easter Day may a layman enter. The Assyrian Church observes a practice or festival unknown to the other churches, called "jayasa." On this day, when the priest is done with most of his celebration, he comes out and looks over the congregation and says aloud, "Who will buy jayasa?" Then a layman answers, "I." The priest asks, "How much?" and the layman replies, "An ox," or "a cow." Then the deacon walks down into the congregation. He covers this layman's entire body with a silver mantle and then takes him on his back and proceeds to enter into the kanki, but before entering the priest begins to read from a manuscript. He warns the deacon and the layman that they cannot enter there, that God has cursed the human race and driven it out of the Garden of Eden, that the angel stands with a sword in his hand at the door of the Garden in order that no one may enter. Then he strikes at the head of the layman with a little stick. The deacon argues with the priest, citing the fact that Christ has triumphed over sin and has removed all barriers between man and God. After a ceremony lasting fifteen minutes, the deacon triumphs and the priest opens the door of the kanki for the layman. The layman is carried on the back of the deacon into the holy of holies, face covered and silent. Only one man can enter this place during the year.

THE RITUALS

The Assyrian kudasha (rituals) for Communion are as follows: (a) the apostles' ritual, which is only in use in the Assyrian Church; (b) the ritual of Theodorus; (c) the ritual of Nestorious. Every kudasha or ritual, is said at a particular season of the year.

During the communion service the priest is assisted by two deacons, and all must be in the act of fasting. The order of prayer is very long, lasting from three o'clock until six o'clock. The people of the town who go very early to the church stand during the entire long service. They generally remain quiet until the priest comes from the kanki with two deacons, one on either side.

One deacon holds the communion bread so that the priest may minister, the other deacon administering the wine. Hitherto the public had patiently stood for long hours, but at the sight of the priest each hastens to receive. Consequently, there is much confusion and lack of decorum. At times the priest stops giving communion to calm the congregation.

After the men have made their communion, then come the boys, followed by the girls and then the women. The women come forward quietly and gently. They stand during the service in the rear of the temple. They are generally the first to come and the last to leave. Before the Korbana (Communion), the priest reads the Khosaya (Absolution). The people do not confess their sins, but the priest prays and asks God for the forgiveness of his people. At times you can see men who refused to speak to one another for months, as they approach the priest, kiss each other and then make their communion.

BOOKS

The Assyrian Church is known as the treasure house of ancient literature. The books are written in the language which Christ spoke, and most of the documents go back to the second and third centuries. Before the printing press was invented, the number of manuscripts in Syriac surpassed that of all other countries together. Unfortunately, owing to constant persecutions by the Kurds, much of this valuable literature has been destroyed. Parts of it have been collected by the missionaries, and copies are found in almost every museum, library, and place of art; other treasures exist which have not been discovered by outsiders. When there are persecutions in Kurdistan, the priest hides the manuscripts in vaults made in the crevices of the church. A stone is placed before the opening and no stranger can then tell where the manuscripts are hidden. At times the priest is killed or dies suddenly, and the secret of the documents is buried with him. Occasionally when churches are undergoing repairs, workmen come upon these books, and, in many instances, hundreds of valuable manuscripts which the Nestorian priests had accumulated have been recovered.

CHAPTER VII

NESTORIAN MISSIONS IN THE FAR EAST

WHEN we think of the struggles of missionary organizations of today in their effort to carry the Gospel to the Far East, it is hard to believe that there was a time when the Gospel was taught throughout the greater part of Asia. Yet from a very early date, even while the East Syrian Church belonged to the Patriarchate of Antioch, we find Syrians expressing their faith through missionary effort. While the Western Church devoted its attention to dogmatic discussion, the East undertook the spreading of the Gospel. As early as the fifth century there were Bishops in Teheran, Ispahan, Khorasan, Merv, and Herat. In the sixth century we hear of their work in Ceylon, near Bombay, and at Malabar. In the eighth century they are in Egypt and Cyprus. Later we hear of them in Afghanistan, Turkestan, and Siberia. Not only did they carry the Gospel with them, but also education. Throughout Asia the term Salabi, from the Arabic term Salab (a cross or crucifix), became the title of a learned man. An Assyrian friend bearing this name claims that it is the same as "Chelebi," the title of the Grand Master of the Order of the Dancing Dervishes at Konia, who until recently invested the Sultans with the Sword of Osman.

The coincidence of the opening of the trade routes into Farther Asia with the ascendency of the Nestorian Church offered a ready outlet for missionary effort. The Nestorians eagerly seized this opportunity. Marco Polo tells us that in his day the trade routes from Bagdad to Peking were lined with Nestorian chapels.

The earliest efforts in China date from 635. In 636 we learn that one A-lo-pen from India won the ear of the Emperor, who listened attentively to the reading of the Sacred books and, upon hearing their message, granted permission for public preaching of the doctrines.

The Moslem persecutions of 699 and 813 did not check the zeal of these earnest missionaries. In 1265 there were twenty-five Asiatic provinces, with seventy Bishoprics. These were tolerated and to certain extent encouraged by the Caliphate, but finally were swept away by the fury of the hordes of the Great Khans. They suffered from the onslaught of the Khans, not because the Khans were hostile to Christianity, but because the Christians stood in the way. In fact, individual Nestorians were employed by all the Great Khans as Ministers of State and as trusted physicians.

Later we find the Kahns marrying into Christian families. Hulagu Khan, a grandson of Jenghiz Khan, is said to have been espoused to Abagha, daughter of the Emperor Michael Paleologos. Hulagu died before his marriage and Abagha married his son. Toktu Khan, of the Golden Horde, married the daughter of Andronicus II and later Uzgeg, Khan of the Golden Horde, married the daughter of Andronicus III.

For the next fifty years the prestige of the Nestorian Patriarch rapidly declined, as the influence of Islam extended eastward. About 1385 came the blighting forces of Tumurlung

(Tamerlane), which swept away every Christian institution, driving the remnant of the Nestorians to the mountains of Kurdistan. Even here in their weakness we find them taking thought of China. Toward the end of the fifteenth century the Patriarch Simon sent a Metropolitan into China, and as late as 1502 we learn of a mission of four Nestorian Bishops.

For a long time legends centered on Prester John, a king and priest, to whom the thoughts of the West turned in hope of an alliance against the nomads of Islam. This title, which is traced to both Turkestan and Abyssinia, is in all probability rightly ascribed to the ruler of the Kariat tribe of Turks. In the eleventh century Mar Abhdisho, Metropolitan of Merv, in Khorosan, wrote to the Patriarch of the conversion of Unk-Khan, King of Kariat. Unk-Khan asked for priests. The Metropolitan was instructed to send a priest and a deacon. Unk-Khan was baptized, assuming the baptismal name "John" and modestly taking the title presbyter or prester, a title which was supposedly carried by his successors until the end of the fourteenth century.

One of the most interesting outgrowths of this contact with China was the elevation of a Mongolian from East China to the Patriarchate, and the mission of his companion to the Western churches. Two Mongols, Mark of Kung-Chang and Bar-Soma of Peking, entered the priesthood and embraced monastic life. They became inspired with a desire for a pilgrimage to the Holy places. Despite opposition from friends and civil authorities, they set out upon a journey, the hazards of which scarcely can be realized in these days. After many hardships they reached the Patriarch Denkha, in Persian

MISSIONS IN THE FAR EAST 67

Azerbaijan, and accompanied him to Bagdad. They were pressed into the service of the Patriarch and undertook an important mission to the Khan Abgha. Mark was elevated to the Metropolitinate under the title of Yahb-Allaha (given by God), and later was chosen to succeed Denkha as Patriarch. At a later date the Khan Argon desired to enter into friendly relations with the West through the Pope, in the hope of establishing an alliance against the Egyptian Mamelukes. Yahb-Allaha was asked to arrange for the mission and appointed Bar-Soma. This gave great satisfaction to Argon, who appreciated the favorable impression likely to be created by a Mongolian Christian. Bar-Soma sailed in 1287 from Georgia across the Black Sea, visiting Andronicus II, the father-in-law of Toktu-Khan. Thence he proceeded to Italy and met the College of Cardinals who were assembled to fill a vacancy in the Papacy. Later he visited Phillip IV of France, and Edward I of England, who was at that time himself visiting his French possessions. Before his departure, Bar-Soma administered the Communion to Edward. Returning to France, he met the newly elected Pope, Nicholas IV. He took part in the ceremonies at Rome during the Holy Week and Easter, 1288, and received the sacrament from Pope Nicholas.[1] He returned home with greetings and gifts for the Khan and the Nestorian Patriarch.

Gradually all the activities of the Nestorian Foreign Missions ceased and nothing remained

---

[1] The Assyrian records state that Bar-Soma administered the sacrament to the Pope. This is the usual custom on such occasions.

to tell the tale except the numerous Syriac inscriptions on the tombs in Turkestan and Siberia.

The most famous of these monuments is the so-called Nestorian tablet discovered in Changan, the modern Sianfu China, in the seventeenth century (1625), by Jesuit missionaries. This tablet was erected to the glory of the Christian religion in 781. The inscription is mostly in Chinese, with annotations in Syriac. Soon afterward the city was destroyed and all trace of the tablet lost for centuries. It is a remarkable fact that the Syriac letters, following the Chinese custom, are in vertical lines.

The best translation seems to be that of P. Y. Saeki, a Japanese, of Waseda University, Tokyo[1]. The inscription begins: "Eulogy on a monument commemorating the propagation of the Luminous Religion, with a preface to the same, composed by Ching-Ching, a priest of the Tach-in monastery."

The opening sentence reads:

> Behold! there is one who is true and firm, who being uncreated is the origin of origins, who is ever incomprehensible and invisible, yet ever mysteriously existing to last of the lasts; who, beholding the secret source of the origin, created all things, and who, bestowing existence on all the Holy Ones, is the only unoriginated Lord of the Universe—is not this our Aloha the Triune, mysterious person, the unbegotten and true Lord?

Some passages seem rather modern. Referring to the religion of the world before the Incarnation, the tablet states:

[1] *The Nestorian Monument in China*, P. Y. Saeki, London, S.P.C.K., 1916, p. 162.

Three hundred and sixty-five different forms (of error) arose in quick succession and left deep furrows behind. Some thought to call down blessings (happiness or success) by means of prayers and sacrifices; others again boasted of their own goodness, and held their fellows in contempt.

As a contrast to this picture, it states:

Therefore our Trinity being divided in nature, the illustrious and honourable Messiah, veiling His true dignity, appeared in the world as a Man; angelic powers promulgating the glad tidings; a virgin gave birth to the Holy One in Syria; a bright star announced the felicitous event.

Concerning the introduction of Christianity into China it says:

In the time of the accomplished Emperor Taitsung, the illustrious and magnificent founder of the dynasty, among the enlightened and holy men who arrived was the most virtuous Olophon, from the country of Syria. Observing the azure clouds, he bore the true sacred books; beholding the direction of the winds, he braved difficulties and dangers. In the year 635 he arrived at Chang-an; the Emperor sent his Prime Minister, Duke Fang Hinen-Ling; who, carrying the official staff to the West border, conducted his guests into the interior; the sacred books were translated in the imperial library, the sovereign investigated the subject in his private apartments; when becoming deeply impressed with the rectitude of the religion, he gave special orders for its dissemination.

70 *THE OLDEST CHRISTIAN PEOPLE*

It concludes:

> This was erected in the second year of Kienchung, of the Tang Dynasty[1], on the seventh day of the first month, being Sunday.
>
> Written by Lu-Siu yen, Secretary to the Council, formerly Military Superintendent for Taichan; while the Bishop Ning-shu had the charge of the congregations of the Illustrious East.

There are two lines in Syriac in the Espangelo characters, written vertically, as follows:

> Adam, deacon, Vicar Episcopal and Pope of China.
>
> In the time of the Father of Fathers, the Lord John Joshua, the Universal Patriarch.

The tablet also contains the names of sixty-seven missionaries written in Syriac, and sixty-one written in Chinese.

While Renan and Voltaire scoff at this monument, recent historical research upholds its authenticity. Direct confirmation is found in a Buddhist publication in Chinese. A Buddhist priest Prajna travels from Central India to China. "He arrived in China and came to the upper provinces (North) in 782 A. D. He translated together with King-Tsing, Adam, a Persian priest of the Monastery of Teitsin, the Satparamba-Sutra from a text."[2]

Other interesting discoveries were made in 1908, when Paul Pelliot discovered eleven kinds of old books. Among these were some Nestorian writings. Two of them were "The Nes-

[1] 781 A. D.
[2] Quoted by Saeki, p. 72.

torian Baptismal Hymn to the Trinity" and "The Praise-Sutra or Nestorian Book of Praise, Dedicated to the Living and the Dead." This latter corresponds to the Nestorian Diptych or mementos of living and dead benefactors.

One can gather some idea of the extent of the influence of Western religions in China from the Imperial Edict promulgated in 845, ordering the destruction of Buddhist temples and monasteries, and then continuing:

> As to the monks and nuns who are aliens and who teach the religion of foreign countries, we command that these—over three thousand—from Ta-ch-in (Syria, i. e., Nestorian) and Mutrufu (Mohammedan) return to secular life and cease to confuse our national customs and manners.[1]

In 846 a letter to the Emperor Wu-tsung places the number of these teachers at two thousand. We can gather from this how many in number would be the converts who would require from two to three thousand teachers. Inasmuch as the Nestorians are mentioned first, they were presumably the more numerous. There must therefore have been at least eleven hundred Nestorian teachers at that time.

One naturally wonders what became of their converts. Part of the explanation may lie in the large number of Mohammedans found in China during the past century—about twenty-one million—a number which cannot be accounted for by the usual laws of increase.

It is quite possible, since they were fellow sufferers and racial kin, that the outlawed teachers banded together in one body, which in time

[1] Quoted by Saeki, p. 47.

was dominated by the Mohammedans. This is not so difficult to comprehend. When the Mohammedan is separated from the centers of Mohammedan fanaticism, his sources of antagonism to Christianity, if any, will be of a political rather than a religious character. We find Queen Elizabeth and Sultan Murak Khan discussing an alliance on the ground of their common hatred of idolatry and worship of the Blessed Virgin.

Even this assumption does not account for the disappearance of all the Nestorians. Chinese and Japanese students have found an explanation in the Christian character of the largest of the great secret societies, the Chin-Tau Chiad, "The Religion of the Pille and Immortality." The chief prophet of this society is Lu Yen (born 755 A.D.). He was a profound and voluminous author who wrote extensively on the subject of immortality. Unlike other Chinese writers, his approach to the subject was a moral and spiritual one. He claimed that his inspiration was derived from the greatest of the "Eight Immortals" who had lived seven hundred years before him. He does not give his name, but speaks of him as "The Warning Bell that does not use Spiritual Force," "The Quiet Logos," "The King of the Sons of God," "First Teacher of the True Doctrine of Immortality," and "Teacher From Above." All these seem to point to Jesus of Nazareth.

Professor Saeki, in an exhaustive study, identifies Lu-Yen with Lu Hsi-Yen, the penman of the Nestorian inscription.

Many investigators report the influence of Nestorian monastic life in the Secret Religion of Thibet.

MISSIONS IN THE FAR EAST

We are justified in thinking that not only has the Nestorian Church played a large part in the past, but has laid the foundation for a wider extension in our own day of Christianity in China.

CHAPTER VIII

RISE OF ISLAM AND THE ARABIAN CONQUEST

WHILE the Christian Church was torn by internal controversy, Christianity encountered a new and more formidable opposition in the rise of Islam. The rapid expansion and growth of Islam cannot be paralleled. No other religion has succeeded in becoming so dominant during the lifetime of its founder. Within forty years of its appearance in the East it unified the roaming tribes of Arabia into a confederate state and abolished idolatry.

The very first encounters between the Arabian forces and the imperial armies will serve as satisfactory examples of the vigorous power of this new faith. They reveal the fervor of its adherents, who feared neither the arrow nor the sword, but marched willingly to battle, ready to give their lives for their religion. Nothing proved able to restrain these nomadic Arabs from carrying out the program of their new faith. In Syria, within the first century of the Mohammedan era, city after city fell before the advancing hosts of Islam. The Roman garrisons lowered their standards, and steadily retreated northward toward Constantinople—humiliated, fearful, unable to make successful resistance. Christian churches were being constantly converted into Mohammedan mosques, and the cross supplanted and replaced by the crescent.

ISLAM AND ARABIAN CONQUEST

During this period of conflict between the Arabs and the Imperial armies, a large force under the command of Syad, one of the famous Arabian generals, was dispatched into Assyria and Mesopotamia. The Persians made every effort to check the advance of the Mohammedan armies, but all these attempts failed to weaken the spirit of the warlike tribes of Arabia.

The Arabian conquest of Persia was different, however, from that of Syria. In this instance the Mohammedans were trying to stamp out Paganism, and therefore they enlisted on their side forces of the Eastern Christians who had been persecuted by these same Pagans. By these Christians in Persia the advent of the Islamic army was universally regarded as the hope of salvation from the tyrannical rule of Paganism. On the other hand, its conquest by Islam caused but little change in the political and spiritual institutions of the land. The traditions were the same. The Arabians conquered Mesopotamia, but in reality they were conquered by the highly developed civilization of the land. The Arabs were very tolerant toward their Christian subjects, especially toward the Nestorians, to whom they granted certain special privileges, exempting them from military service and from the tributes which they levied on other conquered races. A documentary decree was issued by Mohammed and written by Ali, his son-in-law, in which he promises to the Nestorians protection and special privileges at the hands of his followers. This document was given to the Nestorian Patriarch Essvo Yabh toward the end of the seventh, and was treasured by the Patriarchal family until the end of the last, century. It is now said to be in the Ottoman Museum in Constantinople.

Nestorian writers, philosophers, theologians, scientists and literary men were employed by the Arabian Caliphs and their courts. The Arabians, for all they were so powerful and making such rapid progress, lacked education. Their language was a mere dialect unfit to express the intellectual and political ideals of the great empire which they were rapidly building. Nestorians were employed to translate into Arabic the works of the Greek philosophers which were current in Syriac. Schools of philosophy and medicine were opened in many of the large cities. Most of the teachers were Nestorian Christians.

An important factor in the history of our civilization which should be recalled is that Greek philosophy and Greek culture, even though they existed centuries before and after the Christian era, did not contribute much toward religion and progress in the East, nor even in the Western world, because they were not understood. Classic learning grew out of the zeal of the Assyrian writers who wrote the commentaries on the works of the Greek philosophers, and finally succeeded in harmonizing Greek philosophy with Semitic thought and science with religion. For example, healing was done by the priests, but when medicine was introduced the priests offered to the patient both medicine and prayer. At this period the Nestorian libraries contained more manuscripts of classical and scientific learning than any others throughout the world. Note how Greek thought was transformed by the Nestorians, given to the Arabs, and through the genius of the Arabian empire carried to the far corners of Africa, Spain and Europe, and then

ISLAM AND ARABIAN CONQUEST 77

back again to Greece. Thus it encircled the heart of the world and became the greatest contribution which the Nestorians and Arabs have made to mankind. Most scholars will admit that as far as the beginnings of modern chemistry, gun-powder, the compass, medicine, philosophy, and even in some measure, theology, are concerned, much is due to the combined labors of the Nestorians and the Arabs.

It must be confessed that the reign of the Arabs marks one of the most peaceful and prosperous periods in the history of Eastern Christianity. The freedom bestowed at this time on Christians cannot be paralleled in any other period. Harun-Al-Rashid, one of the best Caliphs of the Arabian Empire, was loved by both his Christian and Moslem subjects. A man of exalted ideals, he never wasted time in luxurious living like his predecessors. Even though busy with the war with Greece and with internal troubles, his reign was an excellent one. His prime interest in life was education.

Unfortunately, the Arabian rule ended with the fall of Bagdad before the power of the Mongol armies under Hulagu Khan, 1268 A.D. At the outset the Mongols were very friendly toward the Nestorians, reserving their hostility for Mohammedanism, which they regarded as the state religion of the countries which they had conquered. Christianity made a good impression on the adherents of Buddhism and other Chinese religions because of a certain similarity in their teachings. This was not true of Mohammedanism, which had become materialistic and intolerant. Several Mongol princes embraced Christianity and tried to stamp out Mohammedanism.

78 *THE OLDEST CHRISTIAN PEOPLE*

Thus, the golden days under the Khans marked wonderful expansion and success in the Nestorian Church. Nestorian missionaries went among the Mongols, Tartars and Chinese, establishing schools and other Christianizing centers.

Unfortunately, these happy days ended when Tamerlane invaded Mesopotamia and began severe persecutions which crippled the Church and cut off communication with fellow Christians in China, India and other neighboring countries. Tamerlane cultivated the Mohammedans, who were in the majority, and enlisted them in his forces in order to insure the advance of his army westward. So great was the terror inspired by this brutal conqueror that millions of Nestorians in China, India and Tartary became Mohammedans.

At this time the Nestorian Church was strong in the West. During the Papacy of Innocent IV, 1247 A.D., Timotheus, an historian and Metropolitan of Cyprus, attended the Council in Florence and union with Rome was carefully discussed.

During the sixteenth century the weakened Nestorian Church encountered new difficulties and trials from sources within the household of Christianity. In 1551 A.D. a dispute arose in the Nestorian Church concerning the succession of certain candidates to the Patriarchal See. A hostile party, which represented a minority, sent its candidate to Rome, where he was consecrated Patriarch by Julius III, assuming a hitherto unknown title, "The Patriarch of the Chaldeans." The first Chaldean See was at Diarbaker, later at Bagdad, and now at Mosul. This event proved a great menace to Nestorian Christianity and added many burdens to those who stood loyal to the church of their forefathers. Today these Assyrians who surrendered to Rome designate themselves Chaldeans, and are to some degree hostile to the Nestorians. But they still continue to observe the practices and customs of the old Assyrian Church.

CHAPTER IX

RELATION BETWEEN CHRISTIANS AND MOHAMMEDANS

IN ORDER to have a clear understanding of the underlying causes of the present unrest in the Near East, especially in Assyria and Kurdistan, it is necessary to give a brief outline of the conditions existing before the recent war. It is impossible to portray rightly the friendly relations which once existed between the native Christians and their Moslem neighbors without giving a few details.

The tolerance formerly shown by Mohammedan rulers no longer exists and the sacred bonds which were so carefully preserved between Christians and Mohammedans have been broken. It is apparent to any student of the East that the liberties and privileges bestowed on their subjects by the Turkish government have disappeared. Of course, in reviewing the conflicts in Turkish history we cannot fail to note the weaknesses of the Ottoman Empire, its evils and its destructive forces. But Turkey, like her predecessors, has been the victim of the mysterious East. She has never been able to understand her subjects in such wise as to enable her to govern them through their own racial aspirations. To quote from *The Secret of the Near East*,[1] "Turkey has always tried to conquer races far more civilized and far more advanced than her-

[1] *The Secret of the Near East*, by Geo. M. Lamsa, Ideal Press, 1923.

CHRISTIANS AND MOHAMMEDANS

self, and she has tried to uncivilize them and reduce their standards to her inferior level."

In speaking of Turkish freedom, one is reminded of the hundred Eastern Bishops whom the Turkish Government invested with full power to exercise spiritual and temporal authority over their Christian congregations. These Bishops presided at every important public meeting, both political and spiritual. When they appeared in the government courts they were received with military honors, and many of them had liberal compensation from the government for their work. In many contingencies the Assyrian Bishops were the sole authority in their districts, which were almost semi-independent states.

Indeed, in Assyria and Kurdistan, Turks were unknown, with the exception of the few government officials who passed through that region occasionally, collecting taxes, taking the census, or surveying the lands. The Assyrians had their own courts, their own ecclesiastical laws, their own mails (if they ever wrote any letters). The Patriarch was Prince and High-Priest in all ecclesiastical and temporal affairs and the arbiter in litigations. His powers were never doubted and his authority never disputed. On many occasions, even the Mohammedans sought his wise counsel and fair judgment. He arbitrated in a real patriarchal manner, looking on his people as his children and not as his subjects. A few words from his lips were enough to make the guilty confess their faults and prostrate themselves at his feet, asking forgiveness. In such ecclesiastical trials there was no need for lawyers or for clerks and court officials.

82 THE OLDEST CHRISTIAN PEOPLE

To quote from an authority who is considered a well-informed man on the subject:

> Judaism, however, has for centuries ceased to be an Eastern problem, and Christianity would have followed the same course but for the support given to it by the European nations. Mohammedanism, as I have already stated, is the dominant religion of Syria, and it remains strongly militant. To its adherents it is the "true faith" which must tolerate no rival. This does not mean that the Moslems have always been cruelly intolerant of the Christians. No, their history shows that they have been invariably well disposed toward non-militant Christians in their midst. They have been more generous toward Christians, completely under their control, than the Christian sects in the Middle Ages were, or now are, in certain parts of Christendom, toward one another and toward the Jews, and I very much regret to say that the Christian sects in Syria have by no means been a shining example of brotherly love toward one another, and it is rather doubtful whether, if they and the Mohammedans exchanged places, they would be more tolerant toward the people of the Koran than these have been toward them.[2]

The Assyrians as well as other Christians in the Near East have never realized the value of those sacred privileges bestowed on them by their Mohammedan neighbors. The trouble with these Christians was that they were left too free,

[2] *Wise Men from the East and from the West*, Abraham Rihbany, Melrose, London, p. 216.

and their present sad plight has grown out of this freedom.

Eastern Christians were told that the whole world was dominated by Christian nations and that its inhabitants who lived under Christian rule lived on a much higher plane of life. This caused discontent toward Mohammedan rulers. It reminds one of some of the Assyrian impressions of America. They are told that this great country is but a little island, inhabited by five thousand Christian missionaries, whose entire time is given to prayer, fasting and preaching; that the country is ruled by a Christian government, free from all evils and abuses; and that nobody plays golf, drinks whiskey, or smokes. In fact, America symbolizes a new heaven.

Of course, they live in an obscure land—they have no newspapers, no books; therefore, knowledge of the world is limited. They have no idea that in Europe and America banks are robbed and clerks killed in broad daylight, that girls are kidnapped and that hundreds of other "accidents" are happening every hour. Troubles of this character are rare in their country. Kurdish bandits come once in a while and steal sheep. They know these robbers, as they are close neighbors. They expect them every year and realize that this is the only source by which these savage and hostile Kurds can make their living. These Kurds have always maintained a strong belief that work is evil, and that by freeing themselves from hard labor they would be free from "original sin." God had said that "Man shall live by bread alone." The Kurds are the only race who eat and drink, but never work.

These Kurdish robberies are not as disastrous as they seem. Then, too, these people were always engaged in warfare among themselves and at times made alliances with the Assyrians, against the Turks. At other times they attacked the Christians as well as the Turks; they murdered government officials, cut the lines of communication, and claimed to be the landlords of these mountainous regions. Seeing other races working, tilling the soil, they took their share of the harvest by what they considered divine right.

Several times I was held and robbed by these wild bandits. On one occasion they took all my clothes and shoes. They wounded two other Assyrians who offered some resistance. I saw them going among men and women in the caravan, searching everybody, taking their clothing and valuables. One of these bandits was an old Kurd who had collected so many valuables that he was unable to put them all into one bundle to carry away. I went near him and offered him my help in putting the things on his back. He thanked me and told me that, if I could recognize my clothes, he would give them to me.[3]

In order to have a right idea of life and its hardships in Kurdistan, we must remember how in that part of the world the Nestorian people live according to the standards of an older civilization. In truth, they are two thousand years behind their Western neighbors. Consequently they live a simple life, eat simple food, drink cold water springing from the solid rock, work only a few months during the year, and enjoy rest in a land which makes no provision for doctors and dentists, provides no markets for "Father John's" medicine. The people live

[3] This is a personal experience of Geo. M. Lamsa, one of the authors.

CHRISTIANS AND MOHAMMEDANS 85

long, and if there were no Kurds, would grow old and die a natural death.

Contrast this with American life. In 1923 ten thousand people died from automobile accidents in the state of New York alone, and two hundred thousand were injured. Think of the loss of human life in America through mechanical accidents in ships, factories, and by electricity, not to mention bad whiskey! The human losses by accidents in one American city, Washington, for instance, will outnumber all the massacres that ever took place in Assyria prior to 1914. Therefore, if Christians in Turkey had been wise enough, they would have let the matter rest and imagined these wild Kurds were "Fords," and the Turks, reckless drivers. It would have been a far better course for them than futile struggles in behalf of national aspirations. Today they would have been living in their comfortable ancestral home, cultivating land, free from all the miseries and misfortunes of the present time.

Indeed, before the era of Western political domination and the introduction of Western ideas into these Eastern lands, Christians and Mohammedans were more or less friendly, except for incidental hostilities which, at times, broke out between them. In such conflicts, both Christians and Mohammedans suffered alike, as both maintained military forces, and aggressively attacked each other. This enmity, however, did not last very long. After a few weeks of war the Kurd and the Assyrian chiefs would meet together and make peace. Sometimes, the Kurd Sheiks and Assyrian priests participated together in public festivals, eating and drinking together, and discussing tribal affairs. On certain occasions such as Christmas and Easter, prominent Kurds and

Turks came to Christian houses to pay their respects, saying these words: *Aida hingo priozbid!* ("Blessed be your feast!") They sat down on the ground and ate from the same dish as the Christians.

I remember the Kurds coming to my town, borrowing money from the Assyrian, without interest or receipt, and afterwards robbing a caravan on the road; then returning in order to pay their debts promptly. They were always "honest" in their business transactions. They believed that, if they failed to pay in this world, they would have to pay in the next, and that all their property would be "haram," which means unlawful.

Many of these Kurds would gladly prefer to die rather than betray their trust. When a Kurd breaks bread and eats salt with his Christian neighbor, it is a token that he is willing to die for him.

Not many years ago a war broke out between an Assyrian and a Kurdish tribe. The Assyrians murdered more than two hundred Kurds. Some Assyrians were surrounded in a house, finally captured, and brought before their enemies to be tortured in their presence. One of the Kurds who was watching the spectacle recognized one of the captives, and immediately rushed to his rescue. He explained to his compatriots that they must first kill him before they murdered his friend. In the end, he was able to gain his friend's freedom.

Even among these savage people religion plays an important part and accomplishes some things which no government can accomplish.

It is painful to state that the real trouble between the Kurds and Assyrians began when

CHRISTIANS AND MOHAMMEDANS 87

Western schools, with their leaven of Western culture, penetrated into the heart of these regions. Hitherto neither Assyrian nor Kurd had been aware of his racial identity or history. The Assyrians were to some degree civilized, for they had churches, literature, and priests, whereas the Kurds had no such institutions. But they did not escape the influence which religion plays on every Easterner. They believed that Christ was Spirit of God, and that Mohammed was Prophet. They prayed to their God near a spring of water, where they could wash their feet, and put their coats under their knees. When there was no water, they prayed under the shadow of a tree and washed their hands and feet with the soil. They knew nothing about Mohammed or his teachings, for as we have said, they have no literature, not even an alphabet. For this reason the Kurds are the only Mohammedan group which is not fanatical.

The Kurdish attitude toward woman differs from that of the rest of Islam. In other Mohammedan countries, women cover their faces and are not allowed to be seen by men. Among the Kurds, however, women are free and on many occasions entitled to all privileges. Their faces are uncovered. They hunt and fight along with their husbands.

When schools were introduced the Assyrians began to discriminate between themselves and their Kurdish neighbors. They thought of themselves as the descendants of the ancient Assyrians and of the Kurds as their moral and intellectual inferiors.

In time, the Kurds in turn became wise. They were informed by the Turks that they were Mohammedans and descendants of another race.

Thus, two classes of "Wise Men of the East" met together. It is strange, that in the East, when two bandits accidentally meet each other, they hide their weapons; but when two wise men meet, they pull each other's beards. The outcome of it was that the Christian disputed the right of the Kurd to live without working, while the Kurd and the Turk looked upon their neighbor, the Christian, as a European spy, ready to betray his own government and his own civilization.

The Christian, aware of Western supremacy and the power of Christianity, grew impatient and arrogant. He constantly sought Western interference to save him from what he felt to be oppression and degradation.

The Assyrians prayed to God to send Russia to their assistance, as they looked on her as the guardian of the Christian faith. They were soon disillusioned. Whenever Russian influence became dominant in these regions, Nestorian churches and institutions were confiscated by them. Bishops, who held high rank in the Turkish Government and among the Kurdish Chiefs, were persecuted and mocked. Many of them were put in jail and their property confiscated. Indeed, this Christian government was not willing to bestow half the freedom which the Mohammedan states had bestowed on their Christian subjects.

CHAPTER X

THE ADVENT OF THE WESTERN MISSIONS IN THE EAST

WESTERN missionary activities penetrated into the East at a time when the European adventurers, thrilled with new discoveries, were combing continents, islands, seas, and even the oceans, for treasures and commerce. It was a period when European countries had just emerged triumphantly from the bonds of the Roman Church; a time when the seeds of new forces of intellect were sprouting throughout the continent and natives were shaking off the dust of an older civilization. They were ready to revolutionize the whole world. These Westerners, who thousands of years ago had left the East seeking a better climate, better opportunities in the remote lands, now were trying to return to their mother land, crowned with success, and desirous to display their genius and transplant the structure of the civilization which they had developed.

Nearly all great nations who aspire to world supremacy have employed three great forces in their conquests—religion, culture, and commerce. When the Assyrians conquered the East they first tried to dominate the faith of the conquered people. When these conquered races had lost their faith they were easily subjugated and assimilated. In many instances the East has been successful in dominating the world, not so much through her military power as through her ideals and religions. When Pizzarro, the great Spanish General, in his conquest of South America, forced the savage Indians to adopt the Roman faith, moral and physical decline followed. Hitherto these Indians had lived in the open air, free from all superstition, physically and mentally sound, but now they were forced into allegiance to a religion of whose genius they had no conception. They could not understand its traditions nor its real meaning. This resulted in the moral breakdown of millions of Indians in South America. If one travels in many of these South American countries, he can easily detect the differences between the savage Indians, those really converted to Christianity, and those who were forced into Christianity.

The European conquest of the East was based upon different motives. There the Westerners found a people highly civilized, a people with a long history and old traditions. In this case, however, the Westerner did not find treasures such as had rewarded his older adventures. He found, however, economic and commercial opportunities. Hence he decided it was necessary to modify Eastern Christianity and its customs as a means of quickening the sleeping Orientals and making them over into workers in the industrial world.

Thither went the diplomat, the merchant, and the priest, one standing for the power of the Western civilization and supremacy and the other representing Western intellect as manifested throughout the Western industrial world. The third, the priest, filled with the enthusiasm of the words of His Master's command, "Go ye into the world and make disciples of all nations," was there to re-christianize the natives. The advent of the first two forces was received with open arms, as a herald of blessings almost supernatural. The lower and middle classes who had been mistreated by feudal governments hitherto became impressed with the golden opportunities offered to them through Western economic ideals. This was not true of the missionary. He had nothing new to show. His story was an old story; he spoke of a religion which had originated and first been proclaimed in the East, to natives there who treasured traditions of a world conquest for Christ. It was soon noted moreover, that the display of European naval and military forces, to enforce Western customs and manners upon Eastern people, was not in harmony with the message of the missionary.

These fields seemed ready enough for the reception of European culture; but, unfortunately, the Western seed was not in harmony with the Eastern tradition. The whole Western program seemed at variance with the essence of Eastern civilization and social order. It was tearing the natural traditions of the people up by the roots, and the change was so violent and sudden that the natives were unable to digest the essence of Western thought. The whole program was a challenge to the independent states, which one by one succumbed before the power of Western capital, for it drew the Eastern people from peaceful cultivation of the land into the turmoil of industrial activity—from quiet to bustle, from religious interest to self-interest. To the East such progress was construed to mean a break with God, and was looked upon as a curse. Eastern history is one long commentary on the transitory nature of a material civilization.

Following the discoveries made by the Portuguese in East India and the conquest of India by Great Britain, the Roman Church succeeded in carrying on a large missionary program in the Near and Far East. They converted a half million Nestorians in Malabar to the Roman faith. Their later missionary activities extended to the Ottoman Empire and neighboring countries. The Roman Church has since made repeated efforts to bring into its fold the remnant left of Eastern Christianity, especially the Nestorian Church. In the eighteenth century a mission was established at Mosul, and in 1840 another in Persia. These missionaries were able through their personal influence and educational system to win the confidence of the natives and gain thousands of converts.

This aggressive work on the part of the Church of Rome was made possible by the internal weakness of the Assyrian Church. Much of this weakness is due to the divisions growing out of their tendency to jealousy and intrigue. For this reason we find the Nestorian Church of today divided into two factions. The vast majority adhere to the family of Mar Shimun, while a rapidly disappearing minority still treasure the memory of a rival patriarchate in the family of Mar Elia. These factions are in turn opposed by the adherents of the Church of Rome, who in their turn are just recovering from a schism within their ranks, which likewise had resulted in the establishment of two patriarchates.

The actual cause of division dates back to the year 1450. From its earliest days the Nestorian Church in common with the other Eastern Churches elected its patriarch by the common assent of the whole communion, expressed through the Metropolitans and Bishops. In time this led to keen rivalries, resulting in much discord. In 1450 Mar Shimun, the patriarch enacted a law that future patriarchs should be chosen from his family. This ruling existed without dispute until 1552, when three rival claimants to the patriarchal throne arose in different districts. The representative of the main branch of the Shimun family succeeded to the throne and was immediately recognized by the mountain Nestorians. A distant relative disputed his claim and was recognized by the Persian group and became the Patriarch of Urmia. Upon his death the churches of Persia again united with that of Kurdistan. At the same time the churches of the plains chose Saluka, Bishop of Mosul, as their Patriarch. "The latter" says the historian Mosheim, "to support his pretensions more effectually, repaired to Rome and was consecrated patriarch in 1553 by Pope Julius III, whose jurisdiction he acknowledged and to whose commands he had promised unlimited submission and obedience." Although this connection with Rome was not maintained, a rival patriarchate continued in the family of Saluka, the patriarch assuming the title Mar Elia. In 1842 the family succession in this group was broken and the patriarchate which again had come under the control of Rome was transferred by the Pope to another family.

The Church of Mar Elia, although weaker than that of Mar Shimun, had the political advantage of a recognition by a firman from the sublime Porte, which conveyed those advantages that Mohammed is said to have bestowed upon the Nestorian Church. The Church of Mar Shimun, which was confined to Kurdistan, existed by the consent of the people and under the protection of the Emirs of Kurdistan.

The Papacy made many approaches to both patriarchates for over a century. Finally, believing that direct overtures were impossible, a mission was sent in 1681 to the outlying districts. This mission gained a few converts in the vicinity of Diabakir and became the nucleus of the present Chaldean Church. This Church was recognized at that time by Pope Innocent XI, who appointed Yosef as its first patriarch. Under five successive Mar Yosefs strenuous efforts were made to gain over the other patriarchates. In 1778 Mar Elia made his submission to the Papacy and was followed by the Nestorians of the plains. Mar Yosef V, however, continued to exercise jurisdiction over these groups until his death in 1828. The submission of Mar Elia was the beginning of a stormy existence. He was constantly harassed by the intrigues of a cousin and the encroachments of Mar Yosef V. There is little doubt that these troubles were fomented by Papal agents in order to keep Mar Elia entirely dependent upon his superiors, and thus bind him and his church more closely to the Papacy. At his death in 1841, the family of Mar Elia disappeared as a ruling power in both the Nestorian and the Chaldean Church. His immediate successor was Mar Zeyya, who was succeeded the following year by Mar Yosef VI of Diabakir, both of whom were appointed by the Vatican. Followers of the family of Mar Elia still persisted, however, as Nestorians. Bishop Southgate states that he found small groups on the hills surrounding Mosul in 1837.

The Congregationalists and the Presbyterians entered the field in 1835. Their first endeavor

ADVENT OF WESTERN MISSIONS 95

was to help the Greek and Nestorian Churches to preserve their ancient faith. For various reasons, however, they deemed it necessary to introduce the doctrines of their own churches and to create denominational congregations of their own. These early Protestant missionaries were spiritually gifted men who were ready to die for the ideals of their Master. They established colleges and other schools in which various sciences and languages were taught. Their educational system was admired by the natives, whose churches could do little in that line because they were breaking under the strain of constant persecution. Modern education at that time was almost unknown in the East. The priest in many towns was the only one who could read and write. Even his education was confined entirely to the study of liturgical books. The average Nestorian congregation had only one book in its church, and this weighed seven hundred to one thousand pounds.

It is so important that we understand the attitude of the Congregational Church that the quotation of the following extract from *The Day Break in Turkey*, by the Rev. James L. Barton, D.D., seems necessary:

> In order to understand the method employed in planting missions in Turkey and the permanent results following, one must have a clear idea of what the missionaries were attempting to accomplish. Perhaps we can make the subject clearer by stating first some of the things they were attempting not to do.
>
> They were not attempting to plant American churches in Turkey over which the missionaries should preside as pastors,

and which should be under the control and direction of the mission.

They were not attempting to transport into Turkey American churches and American schools, and American customs and dress or anything else that is American.

They were not attempting to plant churches or schools or any line of Christian works which should be perpetually dependent upon contributions from America for their maintenance.

What, then, to speak positively, were some of the things the missionaries were attempting to do in Turkey? It should be stated at the outset that no settled policy was clearly in the mind of any one missionary at the beginning of the work. When the missionary work began in Turkey, no one, not even the officers of the Mission Board, had framed such a policy in detail. All had one vague desire and purpose, namely, to preach the Gospel of Christ to the people who dwell in the Turkish Empire. At the first, as has been stated, there was no intention of organizing churches separate from those already in existence there. It was expected that the missionaries upon the ground would shape and adopt their measures as necessity demanded. Men of broad culture, deep piety, and sound common sense were appointed to the fields, and to them was entrusted the responsibility of evolving a policy for themselves.

When independent Protestant churches were organized in 1846, it seemed the only natural step to ordain over them pastors from their own people. There were several able and well educated Armenians whose fitness for this office was unquestionable. At any rate there were not enough missionaries upon the ground to fill these positions. Perhaps this last fact helped materially in settling the policy of native pastors for a native church. Be this as it may, there was a speedy recognition of the right of the native church to have a pastor of its own from among its own race. This was early recognized as good policy, and was put into operation.

I sincerely believe that the early missionaries had a real purpose in mind and that their endeavor was to uplift the native churches. However, the difficulties arose from misunderstandings between the natives who allied themselves so closely to the missionaries and those who desired to stand as loyal as possible to their dear native church. This was largely caused through the Western education. The progressive elements were rapidly modernizing and looking on their uneducated masses with a different eye. Hence, the menace to the historic churches was so obvious that the Eastern patriarchs had to look on such men not only as missionary converts, but as traitors, and finally banished them from their churches. Consequently, the missionaries were forced to recognize them and organize them into separate communities, thus ordaining them pastors and planting their own churches.

The problem which the American Board had to face was the natural product of lack of unity among Christian Churches and the accompanying impossibility of forming a coördinated program.

No one can conjecture what a unified program, directed with the single aim of reënforcing the morale of native Christians, would have accomplished. There can be no doubt that a unified front is the only successful defense against the advancing power of Mohammedanism in the East. No one can fail to see that by the introduction of so many creeds into the East, the solid unity which made these vigorous Christians so valiant in maintaining their faith is broken, and the racial solidarity weakened. Before the coming of missionaries these Eastern Christians faced only one enemy, the Mohammedan. Now they contend with each other. It is painful to think that the members of a single family, which had always before the introduction of Western creeds worshipped in one Church, should be divided on the question of religion. Today you will find one a Roman, another a Nestorian, and others Protestant Christians.

Our discussion has now reached a point where the question confronts us: Has Eastern Christianity fulfilled its mission? Is it possible for these Eastern Churches to maintain an independent existence and minister to the growing needs of the native people any longer? To answer adequately we must first inquire into the attitude of Western civilization toward that of the East. If the aim of the Christian Church is to Westernize the East, then undoubtedly the old churches must be meshed into the machinery of the West. But if traditions and customs are to be regarded by common consent as a treasured heritage, and if the East has proved the stability of its civilization and its unquenchable zeal for Christ, then, truly, we must search our hearts before we undertake to destroy that which God has treasured through the ages.

Not many months ago, the Rev. Frank Mason North, of the Methodist Episcopal Board of Foreign Missions, asked Archbishop Mar Timotheos: "Can your church become universal, or is it just for your own people?" Dr. North meant well in asking this question. He had lived in the East, and had seen these dying, old Christian communities, and known how their members were still subject to what the American Protestant terms "superstition." But did Dr. North recall that centuries ago the Assyrian Church embraced within its folds people of all races, even Chinese, Turks, and Tartars? He failed to make the right allowance for the fact that if this Christian community is once more given a chance, it will grow to be the one force properly equipped to convert the Mohammedans, since it is the only group of Christian people who have proved that they can live among them and can understand them. Then, too, no American can realize what an influence for good some of these ancient customs and "superstitions" have played in the life of the East. Think of the Assyrian Church, with all its books burned, buildings demolished, institutions closed—and yet the people maintain their Faith! How do they do it? They are able to do it because the enemy of the Church has always been foiled by their customs and so-called superstitions which he cannot destroy. This fact the Westerner does not seem to understand.

The confusion growing out of lack of unity in the mission field is illustrated by the following story. Not so many years ago, an English missionary, Rev. W. A. Wigram, traveling in Kurdistan, was amazed by this strange incident, reported to him by an Assyrian deacon. During a very heated religious debate between the Kurds and Assyrians, an attempt was made to decide which was the best religion, Mohammedanism or Christianity. While the discussion was going on, a cock crowed three times; "Dina deney Issa" (The religion of Jesus). The owner of the bird took cognizance of the incident, and reported it to the Sheik. He told the latter that either he must become a Christian, or he must kill the cock for his heretical utterances. The clever Sheik, after giving the matter ample consideration, came to this very fair judgment. He told the owner of the bird that he need not kill it, but neither need he become a Christian. He explained that there are three hundred religions in the world, each one claiming to be founded by Jesus. While the cock had proclaimed the religion of Jesus, the bird had failed to tell which one of these he meant.

Ultimately, the bird's neck was saved, and he was kept in the Sheik's house and regarded as a sacred possession.

The Anglican Church established no contact with the Nestorian Church until 1836, when the American Episcopal Church sent the Reverend Horatio Southgate, who afterwards became Bishop of Constantinople, to investigate the necessity for missionary work in the Near East. The same year the Royal Geographical Society, and the Society for the Promotion of Christian Knowledge sent Mr. Ainsworth and Mr. Kassam to Kurdistan to study conditions. On their return, they placed before the Society for the Propagation of the Gospel the direful need of

ADVENT OF WESTERN MISSIONS 101

the Christian Church in that region. In 1842, the Society, with the consent of Archbishop Howley, sent the Reverend George P. Badger and Mr. G. P. Fletcher on a mission to Kurdistan. They were recalled, however, the following year. In 1868 Mar Rouel Shimun was so distressed by the prospects of his Church that he sent a distressing appeal to the Archbishop.

The sudden change in the educational policy introduced by the Presbyterians and Congregationalists was viewed as a challenge to the orthodoxy of the native churches. The Assyrian Patriarch Mar Rouel believed that the ancient Church was endangered. On one hand it was losing to the Roman Church, and on the other to Protestantism. The Patriarch then made the above-mentioned appeal to the Archbishop of Canterbury for immediate help. The Archbishop, after careful consideration, in 1876 sent the Reverend E. L. Cutts to make a survey. The missionary, impressed by the loyalty of these people to the Faith, brought back a favorable report, which was published under the title "Christians under the Crescent in Asia." Archbishop Tait set about the establishment of a mission for the preservation and uplift of the Assyrian Church and people. The first station was in Persia, because for economic and political reasons the Turkish government did not allow missionaries to settle in Assyria. Finally, in 1881, the Reverend Rudolph Wahl, an Austrian by birth, but in the Orders of the American Episcopal Church, was sent out by the Archbishop. He was recalled in 1885. The following year the Archbishop of Canterbury's Assyrian Mission was formally opened under the direction of the Reverend W. H. Brown and the

Reverend Arthur J. Maclean. The education offered by the Anglican missionary was in no way comparable to the high standard of the Presbyterian and Roman Catholic institutions; but the friendly attitude of the Anglican mission created a strong bond between the Assyrian and the Anglican Churches. Through the activity of this mission many ancient books were printed. Thousands of men who came from mountainous regions, untouched by Western civilization, acquired an education. For nearly half a century this mission stood as a civilizing institution in the heart of that region and exerted a tremendous influence over the people. Here nearly all the Assyrian priests, bishops, and other ecclesiastical authorities of the last decades received their training.

This work was constantly augmented, and scholarly men offered themselves to the work of the Mission. Later on, the Assyrian Church was strengthened by the appointment of Anglican Sisters for work among girls. Interesting to Americans is the participation of the Episcopal Church of America in this mission field, and the winning over of the Reverend Yaros M. Neesan, an Assyrian, a graduate of the General Theological Seminary in New York and in Episcopal Orders.

In 1897 the mission met grave reverses coincident with the death of Archbishop Benson. One of the writers of this book had planned to enter the Mission that year but was prevented by the depressing conditions which prevailed. *The Church Times,* of June 4, 1897, quotes the following from the annual report:

> The Archbishop of Canterbury closed the meeting with a few earnest and stirring

ADVENT OF WESTERN MISSIONS

words. He said it was the mission of the Church to convert the world; the Church had no choice about it. It was the command of their Lord and Saviour. Then, from her relation with all parts of the world, God, in His providence, seemed to have set the task especially to England of bringing the Gospel to the nations. Further, they were bound in this mission work to adopt such opportunities as they had. They sent missionaries to the colonies; they sent missionaries to the heathen lands. In both cases they sent out men of their own, and the converts were to be members of the Church of England. But it was quite impossible to maintain that the one way of being Christians was to become members of the Church of England. They could not maintain that their own form of Christianity must be imposed on all alike. Different nations would need different modes in their worship, in their constitutional arrangements, in their discipline. And there was now the question of getting hold of some ancient churches already existing, and getting them to do some part of the work. Here were people who came to them beseechingly, whom the Church of England had not singled out, but who had singled out the Church of England; people who came saying, "We are ignorant, we know it. Send us teachers." Now, if they could restore this ancient Church to its pristine strength, it would have opportunities of reaching Asiatics in a fashion which English people could not imitate. There were people who had held fast to the faith

104 THE OLDEST CHRISTIAN PEOPLE

ever since Apostolic days, whose liturgies, it might be, went back even to the time of the Apostles, who had stood their ground in the face of Islam on every side, and who, in spite of much persecution, had still held fast to the main doctrines of the faith. Well, teachers had been sent. There were now about one hundred village schools in the Mission, with some two thousand scholars. And there was a theological college for the instruction of the ministers of the ancient Church. It was very likely, he thought, that more work of this kind might open up for the Church of England, that, for instance, they might one day be doing for Egypt what they were now attempting in Eastern Syria.

The Archbishop's speech was listened to with the closest attention, and frequently interrupted with hearty cheers.

After the war it became necessary for the English Church to withdraw for a time from its work among the Nestorians. The American Church, which had never lost its interest in the Ancient Church of the East, arranged with the Archbishop for the establishment of an American unit. As a result, there was formed in America an American Committee of the Archbishop of Canterbury's Mission. In July 1925, the Reverend John B. Panfil and Mr. Enoch Applegate were sent to Mosul. Father Panfil was commissioned to promote friendly relationships with the Church authorities and to assist in the education of candidates for the priesthood. To Mr. Applegate was assigned responsibility for the education of the children. A number of young men have been gathered by Father Panfil and the prospect

ADVENT OF WESTERN MISSIONS 105

of an enlightened priesthood is now opening before the Assyrian Church.

Reports from recent investigations made in the field reveal a picture of an increasingly desolate Church. It is learned that about fifteen thousand Nestorians have returned to the district surrounding Lake Urmia, among whom there is not a single Nestorian priest. All their churches and ecclesiastical books have been totally destroyed. Instructions have been forwarded that a priest be sent to these people as soon as possible.

A flourishing day school has been maintained for the past two years by funds raised by the Episcopal Church. There is besides in Mosul a Presbyterian Mission, now conducted by the Reformed Church of America. While its work is of a very high grade, this, however, as a denominational mission, does not aim at rehabilitating the ancient Church. The Nestorian School has been completely reorganized and fully manned with an efficient corps of teachers. Applications have been made for schools of this kind in many villages, and teachers have been nominated. It is hoped that in a short time schools may be established in all these centers.

In the meantime, the resources of the missionaries have been taxed in dealing with the deprivations following the famine and the deportation of Nestorians from Kurdistan and part of the disputed area in the northern part of the Vilayet of Mosul. It must be remembered that although this work is still in its infancy, yet it gives every promise of a helpful future. It is hoped that the Church of England can renew its activities in a very short time. Thus by the united efforts of two branches of the Anglican Communion, the ancient Church of Assyria may be prepared to meet the demands sure to be made upon her in the days of prosperity which, God grant, seem to be approaching for the Kingdom of Iraq.

CHAPTER XI

DURING THE WAR

APPARENTLY the flames of the world conflagration spread from the sparks set flying by Turko-Balkan conflicts. When hostilities began in Europe, Turkey had entered upon a period of peace and tranquillity, after eight years of constant campaigns in Albania, Africa, and the Balkan states, where, in most cases, she suffered severe defeat at the hands of her enemies. For a time her hands promised to let go of these mischief-making activities which were menacing the very structure of the world's civilization. The natural thing for Turkey would have been to remain aloof from war. When the whole world is at peace, that is the time usually Turkey is at war. This time Turkey found it too hard to keep quiet and recuperate from her defeats.

The World War turned out to be such an interesting affair, in a military sense, that Turkey automatically became a belligerent nation and eagerly seized the opportunity to gain fame and to recover prestige by taking part in such an exceptional conflict. In addition, Turkey was not free from alliances and ties with the Western governments. At first these seemed to lead her to cast in her lot with her allies.

While Turkey was preparing for war, most of her subjects knew not the truth concerning the international situation nor the recent Balkan defeats. News had been given out through governmental agencies that the Empire had emerged victorious from both the Italian and Balkan wars. At this time of anxiety and unrest the government was so weak that the forces at the border outposts were utterly inadequate. Turkish garrisons in Kurdistan were withdrawn and disbanded, excepting a few regiments of the 4th Army Corps and a few unorganized reserved divisions. Even these forces were left without supplies. The Kurds were growing hostile. They were as horses left without reins, ready to destroy, plunder, and massacre the peaceful inhabitants of the agricultural districts.

The Assyrians were then dwelling in the fastnesses of the districts of Hakari. Christians and Kurds were living in neighboring towns separated only by hills and mountain passes. Both the Assyrians and the Kurds were aware of the dangerous situation and were preparing for a war of self-protection. Christian soldiers in the Turkish army began to desert their posts. It was almost impossible for them to serve in the army of a nation which for centuries they had looked upon as their moral and perpetual enemy, when that nation declared war against the beloved English, Russian, and other Christian forces who were struggling to make the world safe for peace, to end tyrannical rule, and to liberate enslaved Christian subjects.

Christian leaders were in a dilemma, not knowing on which side national security was to be found. Russian forces had advanced through Persia, and in their encounters with the Turkish army had shown clear signs that they would be victorious. At the time Russia was also massing a large force in Armenia, thus arranging to attack Turkey from the north and the south.

The Turkish government, aware of the warlike spirit of these Kurds and Assyrians, sent propagandists to persuade them either to join the Turkish army or to maintain neutrality. Constant appeals were made to the Assyrian Patriarch Mar Benjamin to maintain his tribes in peace, Turkey guaranteeing to safeguard their tribal interests. However, the Assyrians knew of old that Turkey as a nation never kept her promises and that treaties made by her with Christians were not considered binding. The Turkish agents were assisted by German consuls who endeavored to convince the Christians that Germany would compel Turkey to keep her promises.

Misguided and misinformed concerning the European conflicts, the Christians in these remote regions persuaded themselves that it was to their interest and enlisted on the allied side. Hitherto the Assyrians had waited with patience to see their hope in the protection of Russia realized. Current rumors spread the news that the time would come when Russia would conquer these regions and the long cherished hope of Christian emancipation be fulfilled. Conversation in the streets, in towns, in the general councils, centered around Russia—Russia, the great liberator of Christendom. Hitherto England had prevented Russia from crushing the Turkish Empire, but now England herself had taken arms to end Turkish rule. Such prospects made the peaceful Assyrian tribes cast in their lot with unselfish bravery with the Allies, an event which led to their destruction and dispersion.

When the Turkish government learned that their own subjects had revolted and that there was nothing further to be gained by negotiations, they immediately sent an army to check the rebellion. Turkish authorities at Constantinople arrested the Patriarch's brother, Hurmizd Effendi, a classmate of Mr. Lamsa. They made him write to his brother, who was the temporal as well as the spiritual ruler of the whole Assyrian race, urging him to remain loyal to the Turk. The Patriarch wrote to his brother the following message: "It is better to sacrifice you than to sacrifice the whole race." Hurmizd Effendi was arrested and after long torture was hanged by the Turkish authorities.

Even before the Turkish government had taken any steps to punish the Assyrian tribes, the Kurds were ready for a general massacre of their hereditary enemies. They blocked all the roads and left the Assyrians hemmed in in their mountains and valleys without provisions and arms. The Assyrian Patriarch, who was also commander-in-chief of the tribal army, gallantly led the imprisoned Christians out of the net and brought them safe into Persia. In their hazardous flight the Assyrians fought day and night and defeated the enemy, inflicting upon them heavy losses. Unfortunately, many of the Assyrians elected to remain in agricultural districts, which were largely inhabited and dominated by the Kurds. These suffered severely, and in most instances entire Assyrian towns were wiped out—men, women, and children, even little babies, being put to the sword. When they could not find enough ammunition with which to kill them, the Kurds buried them alive.

The remnant of the Assyrian race which arrived safely in Persia was organized into an army and trained under the command of Russian officers, who recognized the usefulness of these mountaineer fighters and employed them in their campaigns against the Kurds and Turks in northwestern Persia. The tide had turned, and the Assyrian army, coöperating with the Russian forces, made a gallant dash into Kurdistan, stormed all their military barracks, and fortified places and inflicted heavy losses on the Kurds. Had it not been for the restraining influence of the Russian army, the Assyrians would have wiped out the Kurdish population in that region.

While the Assyrian and the Russian armies were still celebrating these victories and were also jubilant over the news of the success of the Russians, under the Grand Duke in Armenia, the sky suddenly darkened. News of the downfall of Imperial Russia and of the abdication of the Czar was flashed to the Russian army headquarters. Anxiety reigned both in the Russian army and among the Assyrian tribes. The situation became so confused that the Russian generals were unable to issue a formal declaration of the program of the new Russian government. At last, the officers were instructed by the Kerensky government to withdraw their forces and make peace with Turkey. Thereupon the Russian battalions, with their morale broken, leaving their arms and ammunition on the way, made a calamitous retreat back home to Russia. Many officers who hitherto had fought side by side with the Assyrian army now were ready to desert their little Christian ally and leave her to the mercy of the enemy. Some orthodox Christian Russian officers continued with the Assyrian army, willing to die with them rather than desert them. They turned over most of their arms and ammunition to the Assyrians, and under the guidance of the Patriarch, reorganized and unified the the Assyrian units and resolutely checked the

Turkish attacks, inflicting heavy losses on the enemy. This conflict had become more than a war. It was a Mohammedan uprising in Persia and Kurdistan against a small Christian community. Once they realized their dangerous position, the Christians relying on their faith in God, resolutely fought the combined Moslem armies, in most instances emerging victorious.

For nearly two years the Assyrian army held northwestern Persia, maintained order, and disarmed the Mohammedan communities therein. They remained firm until the assassination of the Patriarch by Simko, a notorious bandit, broke the morale of the Assyrian army. Simko invited the Patriarch Mar Shimun to his house, and as the Patriarchal party was leaving, the Kurds ambushed an entire Assyrian cavalry force of four hundred men who had come not to fight but as a guard of honor. The entire force, including the Patriarch, was killed, except two men who escaped and carried the news to the Assyrian headquarters.

While the Allied army was making constant progress on the Western front in 1918, the Assyrians were cut off from all the outside world. Persistent efforts were made by English and French military advisors to gain an entrance into Persia. The ammunition of the Assyrians was exhausted and they were facing death either by the sword, or a hazardous journey southward toward the English army, which at this time was operating in the Hamadan region of Persia. They chose the latter course. It was a daring undertaking. Enemy forces had cut off every possible avenue of escape. Thanks to one thousand Assyrian young men who volunteered to attack the Turkish lines at any cost, a road was opened for the refugees. The attack was made under cover of night, under the command of Agha Petros, and heavy losses to the enemy and the capture of many guns and much ammunition were the result. They defeated troop after troop and finally cleared the road for the helpless refugees. The women and children rode, some in little carts, some on mules, with scant supply of bread for their long journey. Days and nights were spent in fear; and most of the women and children died on the road of thirst and hunger. It constitutes the greatest tragedy of the Assyrian race. The flight reminds one of that of the Israelites from Egypt.

Most pathetic was the fate of thousands of Assyrian refugees, chiefly helpless women and children, who had no opportunity to join in the escape. Orphanages, schools, and hospitals were crowded with the sick and wounded. They were left to the mercy of a bloodthirsty enemy. Thousands sought refuge in the American and French missions as the only means of salvation. The Persian army did not respect the French flag. They entered the French missions and slaughtered more than ten thousand refugees, including the entire staff of the Roman Catholic missions. Roman sisters were disrobed and marched in a line, together with Assyrian girls, through the streets, and were murdered after shameful mistreatment and torture.

Meanwhile, the Kurds, hearing that the Assyrians had left all their treasures at the American mission, invaded American headquarters. Thanks are due to Dr. Packard, who stood by the Christians and made every effort to save them. The Kurds ignored the orders of Dr. Packard and other American missionaries, and entered the mission. They seized and murdered a number of the Assyrian men, captured a large number of girls, and looted the entire Presbyterian College. In the interior of the city not a single Christian escaped the wrath of the fanatical Persians, who in their frenzy looked on the murder of a Christian as a virtue.

CHAPTER XII

THE ASSYRIANS SINCE 1918

WE LEFT the Assyrians at Hamadan. The details of their flight and their acute sufferings have been repeated so often that repetition does not seem to be warranted here.

Upon the death of Mar Benjamin Shimun, his nephew, then a boy of about ten, was chosen as his successor in the Patriarchate. The functions of this office in the Nestorian Church are closely similar to those of the Aaronic priesthood. The Patriarch is not only the chief ecclesiastical, but also the ruling, head of his nation. The young Patriarch was with his people during their wanderings and suffered all the privations which they endured.

Events leading up to the recent settlement of territorial rights in the Vilayet of Mosul are so dispassionately and fully stated in the report of the Special Commission of the League of Nations that they deserve quotation in full:

> Immediately after the Armistice a plan was proposed for repatriating the Assyrians, but this proved impossible, largely owing to repeated outbreaks of disorder among the Kurds. As a result of the disturbances at Amadia in July, 1919, the Civil Commissioner suggested to the military authorities that they should evacuate all the Moslem Kurds from the Amadia districts, where there would be room for

the Assyrians assembled at Baquba. In that case they would all be settled in the Vilayet of Mosul. The number of Kurdish families to be transferred was estimated at 2,000. The British Government, however, was unwilling at that time to take any definite decision on this question. The number of Assyrians at Baquba at the end of 1919 was 35,000, divided into two groups consisting respectively of Assyrians from Hakkiari and from Urmia (in Persia).

In the spring of 1920 a certain Aga Petros, an Assyrian mountaineer of the Baz tribe, who had played a not unimportant part as commander of the Assyrian troops during the war, conceived the idea of creating an Assyrian buffer State on the Turko-Persian frontier, while leaving it open to those who preferred to do so to return to their homes in the mountains of the Vilayet of Hakkiar. The execution of this scheme was delayed by the great Arab revolt of 1920, and failed in October owing to the incapacity of Aga Petros and the resistance of the Kurds in the district north of Aqra. In the course of the fighting which took place the Assyrians looted several districts inhabited by Kurds who had taken no part in the hostilities.

After this the Government was obliged to try other measures. It decided to settle the Assyrians tribe by tribe, gradually extending their territory northwards. By the summer of 1921, 7,500 persons had been settled in this way, some in the neighbourhood of Zakho, Dohuk and Amadia and some in the more northeasterly district of

Barwari Bala and Upper and Lower Tiari. A considerable number of Assyrians joined the "levies."

The Government distributed rather more than 1,900 rifles and a certain amount of ammunition among the Assyrian tribes who had returned to their homes north of the frontier of the Vilayet of Mosul.

In April, 1924, the number of Assyrians settled in the territory administered by Iraq and in the region to the north now claimed was estimated as follows: From Persia, 5,000; from the territory subsequently claimed, 14,000; from Turkish Territory, North of the above, 6,000.

Of those in the second group, 7,500 were already settled in the territory claimed at Constantinople. They returned to the south side of the treaty-line in consequence of the incidents which occurred in 1924. It was the British Government's intention to take steps to enable the Assyrians who came from Persia to return to their country.

The relations between the Assyrians and the Moslem peoples are not always as good as they might be, this being, in the view of the authorities, partly due to the lack of tact displayed by the Assyrians themselves, who are of a warlike temper and have somewhat rough manners. In August, 1923, a brawl occurred in the bazaar at Mosul between Arabs and Assyrian soldiers. In the same month hostile demonstrations took place there against a body of about 800 Assyrians who had just been repatriated from Constantinople. Still more serious was the mutiny of two Assyrian companies in the garrison of Kirkuk. This incident which occurred in May, 1924, arose out of a dispute between Assyrian soldiers and Moslem merchants. Despite the efforts of their chief officer and his non-commissioned officers, the men went round the town firing on every Moslem they saw and looting shops and houses. There were casualties, some of them fatal, and British troops had to be sent by air to restore order.

The following are the liberties enjoyed by the Assyrians in Iraq: Their disputes are settled by arbitrators of their own race; their chiefs have an official or semi-official position and collect a regular tithe and a cattle-tax, with the help of police chosen by them from their own tribes. This situation, however, has had to be altered owing to the departure of a large number of them, as a result of the frontier incidents which occurred in the Autumn of 1924.

The family holding the patriarchate is the only Assyrian authority recognized by the British and Iraq authorities.[1]

The British High Commissioner at Baghdad informed the Commission of this Government's intention in case the frontier claimed should be given to Iraq. The territory immediately south of the frontier would be reoccupied by the Assyrian tribes which formerly lived there. At the present time this territory is inhabited by only about 10,500 persons, including 750 Christians. The Assyrians whose homes were north of

[1] This refers to the Shimun family of which the Patriarch is the ruling head. The present Patriarch being a minor, his aunt, Surma de Bait Mar Shimun, who at this writing is visiting the United States, is the accepted head.

the proposed frontier would be settled in the neighbourhood of Dohuk and Amadia —at a certain distance from the frontier. Thus they would not be exposed to the temptation of returning to their homes in Turkish territory and so giving rise to frontier incidents.

The total number of Assyrians to be settled would be only about 20,000 if the Assyrians from Persia returned to their own country. According to later information there is in Russia a considerable number (about 30,000) of Turkish Assyrians who would wish to return to their own homes provided these did not remain under Turkish Rule.

When one of the writers of this book visited Iraq in 1924, he found the condition of the Nestorians pitiable indeed. They are a mountainous people forced to live in the plains. Almost every one of them had become a victim of malaria. Infant mortality had reached an alarming stage. Less than one per cent of the children survived the first year.

The Church was in an equally pathetic condition. The young Patriarch and three bishops in Iraq and a bishop in India (at that time visiting America) were all that remained of the once numerous hierarchy of this ancient Church. Priests are few and uneducated. There was no one with sufficient schooling to become a possible candidate for the Episcopate. If something were not done at once, the Church was in danger of losing its Apostolic Succession.

The young Patriarch was afflicted with malaria and unable to obtain the education necessary for his high office. As a result of this visit, arrangements were made for his education under the direction of the Archbishop of Canterbury, at Saint Augustine's College, Canterbury.

All ecclesiastical books had been destroyed by the Turks and Kurds. Through money sent by the Episcopal Church of America, a printing press had been set up and service books and books of instruction were gradually being published under the direction of a faithful deacon, an old man rapidly becoming blind.

During the last few months conditions have become more acute. The harvests failed last year and the people were facing starvation. Added to this was the horror of the recent Turkish atrocities against the Assyrians who had ventured to return to their old homes, of which mention will be made below.

Recent reports received by the National Council of the Episcopal Church from their representatives tell of the arrival of fifteen hundred deportees in Mosul alone. Their present mode of existence is described in terms which are almost unbelievable. To this is added the statement that in the villages the deportees are more numerous and the conditions worse.

Amid all these trials and sufferings, the people have been living in dread doubt as to the outcome of the decision of the Court of the League of Nations. Happily, this decision has now been rendered. While it does not fulfill all their hopes, it does give them the assurance of peace and protection, and the prospect of more prosperous conditions of living.

CHAPTER XIII

THE ASSYRIANS BEFORE THE LEAGUE OF NATIONS

At the Lausanne Conference the Turks forced a reopening of many of the issues supposedly settled by the Sevres Treaty. Of particular interest to us is the question of the northern boundary of Iraq and the final settlement of the Mosul question.

Immediately after the armistice the Turks had withdrawn from the Mosul district, which was immediately occupied then by the British. At Lausanne the Turks called attention to the unsettled conditions obtaining along the northern border of Iraq, and of the injustice done to the Turks by their exclusion from Mosul, and demanded a readjustment. Provision for an enquiry was injected into the Treaty. Unfortunately, nothing was done at that time by the British in order to press claims for concessions on behalf of the Assyrians. However, in a memorandum, Lord Curzon cited the impossibility of expecting the Assyrians to accept the opening to the Turks of the territory in which they had found asylum, without most bitter fighting.

At the Council of Constantinople, after the British had obtained more accurate data on the topography of the country, and after interested people in England and representatives of the Episcopal Church had brought to the attention of the Colonial Office the direful condition which confronted people reared in the highlands when

122 *THE OLDEST CHRISTIAN PEOPLE*

compelled to dwell in lower miasmic regions, the British government asked for an extension of the boundary northward in order to give the Nestorian Assyrians a home.

Referring to this situation, the report of the Special Commission of the League of Nations states:

> It was at the Conference of Constantinople in May, 1924, that the question was raised by the British Government as an argument for the extension of the frontiers of Iraq.
>
> At the beginning of April, 1924, the British Government had notified the Iraq Government of its intention to demand the cession of a portion of Iraq to the Assyrian territory. At the same time it explained the advantages which Iraq would derive from having on its northern frontier a warlike people united to the Arab state by ties of friendship and gratitude, prepared to guarantee that Assyrians who had not yet settled should be able to acquire, on favourable conditions, some of the abandoned land in the northern districts. The British Government further asked whether the Iraq Government would be prepared to grant all the Assyrians the same local autonomy as they enjoyed before the war under Turkish rule.
>
> The reply of the Iraq Government, which was given on April 30th, was in the affirmative. The new British proposal was explained at the Constantinople Conference on May 19th, 1924, by Sir Percy Cox, who spoke as follows:

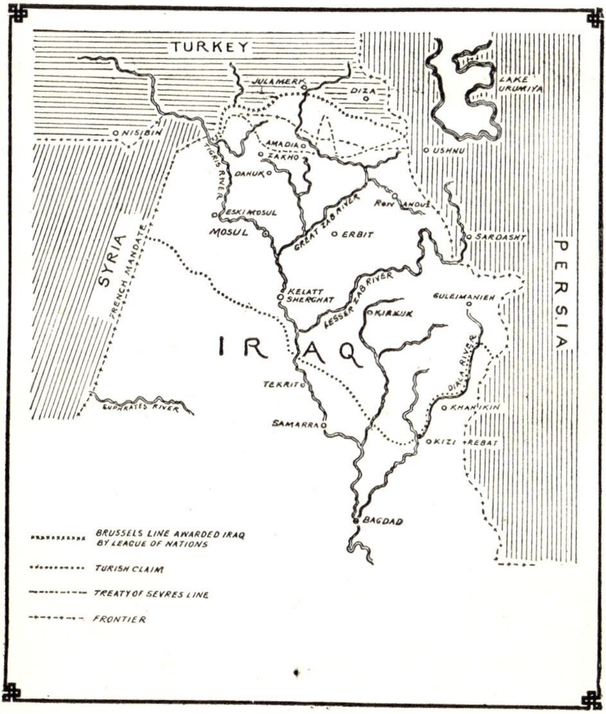
TURKEY
JULAMERK
DIZA
LAKE URUMIYA
NISIBIN
AMADIA
ZAKHO
USHNU
DAHUK
TIGRIS RIVER
ESKI MOSUL
MOSUL
GREAT ZAB RIVER
ERBIT
SARDASHT
PERSIA
SYRIA
FRENCH MANDATE
KELATT SHERGHAT
LESSER ZAB RIVER
SULEIMANIEH
KIRKUK
IRAQ
DIALA RIVER
TEKRIT
EUPHRATES RIVER
KHANIKIN
SAMARRA
KIZI
REBAT
BAGDAD
BRUSSELS LINE AWARDED IRAQ BY LEAGUE OF NATIONS
TURISH CLAIM
TREATY OF SEVRES LINE
FRONTIER

ASSYRIANS BEFORE LEAGUE

"Moreover, since the negotiations at Lausanne were broken off, one problem has gained considerably in importance in the eyes of His Majesty's Government. This problem is the future of the Assyrians other than those of Persian origin. His Majesty's Government feels under the strongest obligation to secure their settlement in accordance with the reasonable claims and aspirations of their race. They have made an earnest appeal which His Majesty's Government cannot regard with indifference, to be established in their former homes under a British protectorate. However greatly such a solution might appeal to Christendom at large, His Majesty's Government cannot, for various reasons, contemplate so grave an extension of its responsibilities. While, therefore, not prepared to respond to their aspirations in full, His Majesty's Government has decided to endeavour to secure a good treaty frontier, which will at the same time admit of the establishment of the Assyrians in a compact community within the limits of the territory in respect of which His Majesty's Government hold a mandate under the authority of the League of Nations, if not in every case in their ancestral habitation, at all events in suitable adjacent districts. This policy for the settlement of the Assyrians has the full sympathy and support of the Iraq Government, which is prepared, for its part, to give the necessary coöperation for giving effect thereto.[1]

Of course, this brought forth vigorous oppo-

[1] League of Nations Document, C 400, M 147, 1925, VII, p. 70.

124 *THE OLDEST CHRISTIAN PEOPLE*

sition from Fethi Bey, to which, in his reply of May 24th, Sir Percy Cox stated:

> The position taken by Lord Curzon at Lausanne has necessarily been modified to some small extent as the result of more detailed topographical data which has recently been obtained, and the earnest need that has been felt to safeguard the future of the Assyrians.

In his reply on May 21st, Fethi Bey had said:

> I should like to add that the Nestorians would still find in Turkish territory the tranquillity and prosperity which they enjoyed there for centuries, provided that they did not repeat the errors which they committed, with foreign encouragement, at the beginning of the Great War.

To this Sir Percy Cox replied:

> Fethi Bey's assertion that the Nestorians would find in Turkish territory all the tranquillity and prosperity which they had enjoyed in the past, provided that they did not renew their wartime activities, did not square with the Nestorians' own views. They had the most vivid memory—entirely at variance with Fethi Bey—of the treatment they had suffered in the past at the hands of the Turks.

The question was finally referred to the League of Nations, at which time (August 11th, 1924) the British offered the following political argument on behalf of the Assyrians:

> In spite of their isolated position in the heart of a country under Turkish rule, the small Assyrian people, in the very early days of the Great War, determined to espouse the cause of the Allies and to seize

the opportunity to break away from the rule of those whom their past history had led them to regard as their persistent oppressors. They endured great sufferings as the result of this decision. They were driven from their own country and died in thousands in their flight to Iraq.

For the time being they succeeded in settling partly in the southern portion of their own country and partly among the Kurds and indigenous Christians of the country immediately to the south of their old habitat.

The British Government feels under the strongest obligation to secure their settlement in accordance with the reasonable claims and aspirations of their race. They have appealed for the establishment, in the whole of their ancient habitat, of a British protectorate.

The British Government has been unable for various reasons to respond to their aspiration in full but has endeavoured to secure them a frontier which would fulfill certain conditions and is now requesting the Council of the League of Nations to establish that frontier. The latter, while fulfilling the requirements of a good treaty frontier, should at the same time admit of the establishment of the Assyrians in a compact community within the limits of the territory in respect of which the British Government holds a mandate under the authority of the League of Nations, if not in every case in their ancestral habitations, at all events in suitable adjacent districts. To draw the line further to the south in this region would, apart from economic and strategic disadvantages, produce such a panic among the Assyrians that they would find no alternative but to resort either to mass emigration or to fight to the death in defence of their ideals. Peace and prosperity upon this section of the frontier would be impossible.

Among its geographical and strategic arguments, the Memorandum in question advances a further reason in support of the proposed frontier—namely, that the warlike Assyrian people were willing to give their loyalty to Iraq on certain conditions and would constitute a valuable frontier community to the Iraq state.

The following part of the Turkish Memorandum of September 6th, 1924, is worthy of mention:

> The Turkish Memorandum of September 5th, 1924, asserts that the British claims to the territory beyond the confines of the Turkish Vilayet of Mosul manifestly exceed the limits of the question which the two parties have agreed to submit to the League of Nations. The Council accordingly will only have to give a decision on the British claim insofar as it is within the limits of the question at issue.
>
> The British Government's proposal to assemble the Assyrians in a compact mass on the frontier between Turkey and Iraq suggests that it is not quite certain whether, whatever may be the wishes of this community, it was really those wishes and not other considerations which prompted this proposal. The artificial grouping on the frontier of the Assyrian who might be util-

ized against the Kurds and who would be animated by a spirit of aggression against Turkey certainly cannot be expected to produce the results that the British Government hopes to obtain—namely, the establishment of a lasting peace in these regions, good relations between Turkey and Iraq and the possibility of a safe existence for the Assyrians.

The commission, while recognizing the necessity of protecting the Assyrian people, could not accept the British suggestion. In the first place they believed it to be an unwarranted introduction of new matters into the problem. It also adds:

> The British authorities also informed the Commission that the future treatment of the Assyrians would depend upon the decision taken with regard to the frontier. If the territory occupied by the Assyrians is not assigned to Iraq, they cannot be granted any local autonomy, because in that case they would not be settled in homogeneous communities. If the frontier were drawn towards the south, thus incorporating in the Iraq only a small part of the former Assyrian territory, it would be impossible to find land for the Assyrian in Iraq. The plan for settling the Assyrians depends on the acceptance of the frontier proposed by the British Government. Even if lands could be found, the Assyrians could not live in the plains, owing to climatic conditions. Other differences of customs between the Arabs and the Assyrians would strain the relations between them, whereas Assyrian and Kurdish customs are much more similar.

The matter is finally dismissed as far the commission is concerned with the following decision:

> In view of the fact that the question of the homes of the Assyrians was not introduced into the dispute by the British Government until the Constantinople Conference, and had never been mentioned in the earlier negotiations or in the Treaty of Lausanne, and since the Assyrian question was the principal argument advanced by the British Government in support of its claim to a frontier embracing a portion of the Vilayet of Hakkiari, the Commission considers that the British Government's claim to this frontier is not justified.

Prior to this the British had stated their intention in a statement summarized by the Commission as follows:

> Another objection to the solution proposed by the British Government resides in the circumstances under which the Assyrians took up arms against Turkey. There is no doubt that this people rose in armed revolt against its lawful government at the instigation of foreigners and without any provocation on the part of the Turkish authorities. It is also established that the conditions of life enjoyed by the Assyrian people within the Ottoman Empire was rather better than those of other Christians, since they were conceded a fairly wide measure of local autonomy under the authority of the Patriarchal House.
>
> Under these circumstances it would hardly be fair to take from Turkey a territory which indisputably belongs to her in order to settle in that territory a people

that deliberately took up arms against its sovereign. The Commission is led to conclude that the most satisfactory solution would be for the Assyrians to accept the offer, made by the Turkish delegate at the Constantinople Conference, that they should be allowed to return to their former homes. In that case it would have to be added that the Assyrians must continue to enjoy the same local autonomy as formerly and that their safety must be guaranteed by a complete amnesty.

This decision, as we shall see later, was confirmed by the Council of the League. As matters now stand there is no immediate prospect of the return of the Assyrians to their ancestral homes. They can, however, gain some comfort from the assurance that the British are on record as pledged to procure a satisfactory home for them. The problem will be simplified by the predicted immigration of the Nestorian Assyrians to the Urmia district of Persia. The Persian government views the mountain Assyrians with more favor than the Assyrians of the plains and is likely to encourage this migration.

For several years it was impossible for any Christian to return because of the depredations of Simko, the Kurd, the murderer of Mar Benjamin Shimun. Now that that menace is removed one looks for the speedy development of a large colony in that district. At the last report about fifteen thousand Nestorians were living near Lake Urmia.

CHAPTER XIV

FINAL SETTLEMENT

IN THE Spring of 1925, when it was feared that the report of the Commission would be adverse to her interest, Turkey began to execute a program of deportation. Kurdish chiefs under whom many Chaldeans lived in serfdom received orders to massacre these defenseless people. Upon their refusal a number of chiefs were put to death.

The 62nd Regiment of Turkish Infantry was dispatched by the Angora government to "clean up" the disputed territory. The manner in which this order was executed equals in horror any of the massacres of modern history.

These acts were reported at the September meeting of the Council of the League, by Colonel Amery. The charges were considered so serious that General Laidoner of Esthonia was commissioned to make an investigation.

The horrors of his report beggar description. The report abounds in tales of cruelty, murder, and unbridled lust, which tell how the inhabitants of villages and towns were driven through difficult mountain passes from their ancestral homes to the plains of Iraq.

The Commission was not permitted to enter Turkish territory to make its own investigation, but made careful investigation through mayors of the villages, priests, and thousands of deport-

FINAL SETTLEMENT

ees. The evidence gleaned of the brutality of the massacres and deportations is indisputable.

To quote from the less horrible portions of the report:

> Turkish soldiers under the command of officers occupied the villages and obtained delivery of all arms, imposed severe fines, demanded women, pillaged houses, and subjected the inhabitants to atrocious acts of violence, going as far as to massacre.
>
> The deportations were conducted en masse and refugees were conducted to a region far from the provisional line. During the deportations several persons fell ill and were abandoned. Others died of starvation and cold, because they were not permitted to carry food and clothing when obliged to leave their homes.
>
> During the inquiry several cases were discovered in which members of families who had taken refuge in Iraq were now in Turkish concentration camps.

"This is the general account given by refugees," says the report, "and we have moreover seen ourselves that all who arrived were in a pitiable condition."

General Laidoner says in conclusion:

> The question of the deportation of Christians is infinitely more important than other charges, for they are causing fairly serious, and easily comprehensible agitation, and nervousness among the Christian population living south of the Brussels line, and the Vilayet of Mosul, and also among the Moslem population of Mosul, which favors the claims of Iraq.[1]

[1] New York *Times*, Dec. 11, 1925.

The Turkish delegation claimed that these massacres were provoked by Nestorians who were attacking the Turks with the connivance of the British government. In this instance, however, the chief victims were not Nestorians, but Chaldeans, who for centuries had lived as serfs of Kurdish chiefs.

Before considering General Laidoner's report, the Council had decided to accept the method of procedure suggested by the advisory opinion rendered by the Permanent Court of International Justice. At its September meeting the Council of the League has asked for a definition of its powers under the Lausanne Treaty. The Court held that: "The decision to be taken will be binding on the parties in the Mosul controversy, and will constitute a definite determination of the frontier between Turkey and Iraq." It was further stipulated that in order to make the decision effective, it must be given "By unanimous vote, representatives of the parties taking part in the voting not counted in ascertaining whether there is unanimity."

After several hours of discussion in which both British and Turkish representatives took part, the Council, on December 3rd, 1925, voted unanimously to accept this opinion.

The so-called Brussels line was considered the most desirable. The Court believed that if they had extended the northern frontier to cover the territory desired by the British for the Assyrians, they would have to enter into a long struggle to dislodge the Turks. On either side of this line the people were well established and their allegiance to their respective governments recognized. If they had extended southward they would have jeopardized the lives of thousands of Christian

FINAL SETTLEMENT

and pro-Iraq Moslems. While this is not a natural border, it is one of high strategic value. It would be impossible for the Turks to cross it with an army of less than three or four hundred thousand. It could be defended by half that number with the aid of the British air fleet.

On December 15th, the Council of the League, by unanimous vote gave Mosul, up to the so-called Brussels line, to Iraq, provided that Great Britain continue her mandate for twenty-five years. The same day this was accepted in the name of England by Sir Austen Chamberlain. Following General Laidoner's report of atrocities no other action could have been taken; otherwise, fifty thousand Christians would have been delivered over to the Turks for like treatment.

When the Turks were summoned before the League to report in accordance with Article III of the Lausanne Treaty, they refused to attend. Finally, December 2nd, the decision was given, making, as we have stated, the Brussels line the northern boundary of Iraq. This is not all that the friends of the Assyrians desired. It does, however, open to them the possibility of a return to the mountainous regions, with an assurance of protection. It seems doubtful if the Turkish protest will lead them to take any warlike action. They recognize that the spirit of Locarno dominates the political mind of Europe, and that circumstances have welded the Near Eastern policies of France and England more closely together. It seems more probable that the thoughts of Angora are more concerned with conditions in Syria than with those in Iraq.[1]

---

[1] During the current month the last chapter of the dispute over the Mosul territory has been written. On June 5th an agreement was signed at Angora by the Turkish representatives and the British delegation. The treaty, among other things,

134 THE OLDEST CHRISTIAN PEOPLE

Industrially the settlement of the disputed boundary question in favor of Iraq opens up wide possibilities for the Assyrians. The Diala irrigation scheme, which will open up to cultivation two million acres between Jabel Hamron and the Kut district, depends upon a dam at the junction of the Tigris and the Naniwhan passes through Kifu. It is planned to devote five hundred thousand acres here to the production of cotton. If we recall that Mosul gave its name to the fabric known as muslin, we will see how naturally the people will take to this industry. Add to this the much discussed oil question and the plans already under consideration for the use of natural gas, and we can picture to ourselves the rise of a large industrial center in the region of ancient Nineveh. Anyone who has dipped his hand in the Euphrates or Tigris will testify to the richness of the alluvial deposits carried in its waters; and one has but to recall the glory of ancient Nineveh, Assur and Babylon to feel assured that the inhabitants of this land have inherited industrial and economical instincts sufficient to enable them to take advantage of this new era of

---

provides for general amnesty for all people in the Mosul region.

By it, Turkey obtains ten per cent of the revenue of the Mosul oil fields, and ten per cent of the Iraq Government's revenue from petrol in Mesopotamia. She is also given the right to sell her interests.

In return for this she accepts the decision of the Court of the League of Nations defining the "Brussels line," with slight modifications in favor of Turkey in the neighborhood of Alimoun, and the maintenance of a demilitarized zone of 75 kilometres on both sides of the frontier. This frontier will be delimited by a Turko-Iraq Commission, presided over by a Swiss. The treaty was signed by Rushdi Bey, representing the Ottoman Government and the British Ambassador, Sir Ronald Lindsay.

This seems to bring to a final settlement the troubles which for the past fourteen years have been assaulting Assyrian and Turk alike.

economic development. It automatically will change the character of the people. The Mystery of the East will disappear; but the people will be saved from misery and starvation.

POSTLUDE

If the authors have been conscious of any program it has been that of directing attention to a people who have long served the world and have given valiant testimony to the vital power of the Gospel of Christ. As the expectation of attracting the Semite to the Gospel of Christ looms larger through the closer contact of nations and peoples, we view with hope the possible triumph of a pure type of Christianity through a steadfastness in faith and devotion even unto death of the Semite type of Christians exemplified by these heroic people.

With the apparent settlement of disputes over the Assyrian homeland and the determined effort of the nations of the world to outlaw the enemies of peace, a new day seems to be dawning for this little priestly nation. We have shown how opportunity has been opened for their return to the mountains, although not to their ancestral homes. We have also shown the opportunities for agricultural and industrial expansion afforded by the contemplated plans for the development of the Kingdom of Iraq. Into these opportunities they will enter. Many will prefer to remain in the mountains, revelling in their freedom and content with the care of their sheep and goats. Others will be attracted to the larger field for industrial and commercial progress in the region of the plains. These opportunities will create a higher standard of living, and thus enable them to adapt themselves to a climate which they now find so devastating. Their history has been one of conquest over adversities and mastery of unfavorable conditions. There need be little fear of their future if they survive the period of stabilization.

To the Church, too, the future seems hopeful, and its mission defined. Their Patriarch is still their national head and around him their hopes cluster. It has been the call of the Church that has led them to endure hardship and resist the temptation of national apostasy. They were reduced to a "small people" and have been a subject people during the past ten centuries. At the same time, they are the most substantial hope for the conversion of Islam that looms upon the horizon today. They are almost indigenous in Turkey, Kurdistan, Persia, and India. Their understanding of the psychology of these people is innate and their approach intuitive. Arabian culture was developed under their leadership and guidance. Mohammed himself recognized his indebtedness to them and spoke to them as to brethren. Even the Turk, as we have seen, was indulgent to them as far as his moodiness and volatile temper would permit. Who could be better fitted for correcting the perversions that turned an impulse to serve the Lord God of Sabaoth into a stumbling block to the people of the East and a menace, for a while, to the whole of Christendom? Hebrew history declares that God does not call great nations to his mighty tasks; but uses small peoples of the world for the confounding of the multitude.

BIBLIOGRAPHY

Stanley, A. P., "Lectures on the Eastern Churches," London, 1863.

Fortescue, Adrian, "The Lesser Eastern Churches," London, 1913.

Janin, Raymond, "Les Eglises Orientales et les Rites Orienteaux," Paris, 1922.

Badger, Rev. G. P., "The Nestorians and their Rituals," 2 vols., London, 1852.

Chabot, J. B., "Histoire de Mar Jabalaha," Paris, 1895.

Labourt, J., "Le Christianisme dans l'Empire Perse sous la Dynastie," Sassamde, Paris, 1904.

Wigram, Dr. W. A., "An Introduction to the History of the Assyrian Church," London, 1910.

———, "Our Smallest Ally," London, 1920.

———, "The Assyrian Settlement," London, 1922.

———, "The Cradle of Mankind," London, 1923.

———, "The Separation of the Monophysites," London, 1923.

Surma de Bait Mar Shimun, "Assyrian Church Customs and the Murder of Mar Shimun."

Menant, M., "Les Yezides," Paris, 1892.

Naw, F., "Receuil de Textes et de Documents sur les Yezidis," Paris, 1918.

Layard (Sir) A. H., "Nineveh and Its Remains," with an account of a visit to the Chaldean Christians, etc., 2 vols., London, 1848.

Southgate, Reverend Horatio (afterwards Bishop), Narrative of a Tour through Armenia, Kurdistan, etc., 2 vols. N. Y., Appleton, 1840.

———, Visit to the Syrian (Jacobite) Church of Mesopotamia, N. Y., Appleton, 1844.

Anderson, Missions of the American Board: Oriental Churches, Boston, 1873.

Percy, Earl, "Highland of Asiatic Turkey," London, 1901.

Bachmann, W., "Kirchen und Moscheen in Armenien und Kurdistan," Leipzig, 1913.

Bevan, Edwyn, "The Land of the Two Rivers," London, 1918.

Porter, R. C., "Giant Cities of Bashan," London, Nelson, 1866.

Naayen, Rev. Joseph O. I., "Shall this Nation Die?" New York, 1921.

Steomes, E. S., "By Tigris and Euphrates," London, 1923.

Poell, Gertrude L., "Amurath to Amarable," London, 1924.

Rich, Claudius J., "Narrative of a Residence in Kurdistan," 2 vols., London, 1836.

Yohanan, Abraham, "Death of a Nation," New York, Putnam, 1916.

Matthews, Basil, "Riddle of Nearer Asia," New York, Doran, 1919.

Saiki, P. Y., "Nestorian Monument in China," London, S. P. C. K., 1916.

Pantheer, G., "L'inscription Syro-Chinoise de S-ngan-fou," Paris, 1858.

Legge, James, "The Nestorian Monument of Hsi-au-Fu," Oxford, 1888.

INDEX

Abgar, King, 25, 27
Abgar, King, letter to Jesus, 26, 27
Abhdisho, metropolitan, 66
Acta, Thomae, piece of Syriac literature, 30 f.
Acta Thomae, traditions of, 28, 29
Adam, deacon, 70
Addi, doctrine of the, 25, 26
Afghanistan, Nestorian mission, 64
Alexandria, theology of, 51
Amedia, town, 118
Andronicus II, Emperor, 65
Anglican Church, mission, 101–106
Animal sacrifice, 21
Antioch, school, 51
Apollinaris, teaching of, 50
Arabian empire, 76
Aramaic, language, 24, 37
Aramaic-speaking people, traditions, 23–f
Ardashir, King, 44, 45
Argon, King, 67
Arians, doctrines of, 50
Assyrian, army, 112–113
Assyrian Church, ceremonies of the, 61-63
Assyrian Church, divisions, 95
Assyrian Church, evangelization of the, 37
Assyrian Church, books and manuscripts of the, 62
Assyrian Church, rituals of the, 61
Assyrian Church, temples of the, 60, 61
Assyrian, deportations, 131
Assyrian, massacre, 112
Assyrian priesthood, influence of, 58
Assyrian priesthood, orders of, 57
Assyrian refugees, 113
Assyrian, remnant of, 119, 120
Assyrians, before the League, 121–136
Assyrians, only Semites Christians, 37
Assyrians, under Russian armies, 110–112

Badger, George P., 101
Bagdad, city, 77
Baquba, 118
Bardazan, 41
Bar-Soma, 67
Benjamin, Mar Shimun, patriarch, 112
Book of Praise, 71
Brown, W. H., 101
Brussels line, 132

Candadian, 53
Canterbury, mission of, 103
Carus, Emperor, 45
Cassius, Roman general, 44
Chalcedon, Council of, 54–56; rejection of, 55.
Chin-tau Chiad, religion in Chia, 72
Christianity, spread of, 38–43
Constantinople, Conference of, 122
Constantius, Emperor, 46
Corzon, L., 121
Cutts, E. L., 101
Cylon, Nestorian mission, 64
Cyprus, Nestorian mission, 64
Cyril, 50

Denkha, Patriarch, 66, 67
Diarbaker, see Chaldean, 78

139

INDEX

Diodore, 51

Edessa, reception of the gospel, 25
Edessa, siege of, 28
Edward II, King, 67
Egypt, Nestorian mission, 64
Eleutheropolis, 27
Ephesus, Council of, 53–54
Ephrem, 41, 46
Episcopal Church, mission of, 104
Esho-Yabh, Patriarch, 75

Florence, Council of, 78
Foreign Missions, Congregationalists and Presbyterians, 95–97
French Mission, destruction of, 113

Greek mind, influence of, 37

Hanan, archivist, 27
Harun-Al-Rashid, 77
Hulagu Khan, 65, 77
Hume, historian, the, picture of Jesus, 27–28
Hurmizd, Effendi, 110
Hymn of the Soul, the, 30–36

Innocent XI, Pope, 94
Irak, 117, 127–128
Islam, rise of, 74–79
Ispahan, Nestorian mission, 64

Jenghis Khan, 65
Jesus, letter to Abgar, 26, 27
Jilu, tribe of the, 21
John, Patriarch of Antioch, 54
John, Prester, 66
Jonah, 22
Joshua, John, Patriarch, 70
Julian, Emperor, war with Persia, 45–46

Kanki, holy place, 60
Khan Abgha, 67
Khebor, river, 46
Khorasan, Nestorian mission, 64
Kirkuk, region, 118

Konoma, person, 51
Kung-Chang, 66
Kurds, relations to Christians, 80–88
Kurds, world war, 109

Laidoner, General, 131
Lausanne, Conference of, 122
Lausanne, negotiations, 121
League of Nations, Assyrian question, 123–130

Maclean, Arthur J., 102
Magi, 23–25
Magians, Magi, the wise men, visit of, 25
Malabar, Nestorian mission, 64
Marduk, 39
Mar Elia, Patriarch, 93–94
Mar-shimon, persecutions, 47, 48
Mar Shimon, Patriarch, 93
Mar Yosef, Patriarch, 94
Mason, Frank, Rev., 99
Mazda, 42
Mervan, Nestorian mission, 64
Mithraism, power of, 38, 39
Mohammedans, relations, 80–88
Mosul, Patriarch of, 93
Mosul, settlement, 133
Mosul, town, 105
Murak Khan, 72

Neesan, Y. M., 102
Nesibin, city, 55
Nesibin, school of, 46
Nestorian Christians, China, 73
Nestorian Church, decline of the, 78
Nestorian, customs of, 57
Nestorian, missions, 64–73
Nestorian, priesthood, the, 57–60
Nestorian, protection decree, 75
Nestorian, tablet, 68
Nestorian, writers, influence of the, 76
Nestorian mission, decline of, 78
Nestorius, controversy, 43–56

INDEX

Nestorius, Patriarch of Constantinople, 50
Nestorius, teaching of, 50, 51
Nestorius, term, 49
Nicholas IV, Pope, 67

Packard, Dr., 113
Palagian, priests, 53
Parthians, war with Rome, 44, 45
Persia, Mohammedan conquest, 75
Persian empire, progress of Church, 41–42
Persian government, attitude toward Christianity, 42–43
Persian government, policy of, 42
Peking, Nestorian mission, 65
Petros Aga, 113
Polo, Marco, 65
Protestant Missions, policy of, 95

Roman, Foreign Missions, 92–94
Romans, war with Parthians, 44–47
Rouel, Mar Shimun, patriarch, 101

Sianfu, city, 68
Sabinus, 25
Sapor II, King, persecutions, 45–48
Sassinides, dynasty, 44–46
Seleucia, Council of, 48
Seleucia, Patriarchs of, 47
Septimus Severus, 27
Simko, 112
Southgate Horates, 100

St. Peter, epistle of, 25
St. Thomas, 28-f
St. Thomas, journey to India, 29–f
Syad, general, 75

Taisung, Emperor, 69
Tamerlane, persecution, 78
Tatian, 41
Teheran, Nestorian mission, 64
Theodore, 51
Theodosius, Emperor, 50
Timotheus, metropolitan, 78
Tokto Khan, 65
Trajan, war with Parthians, 44
Trajan, Roman wars, 19
Turkey, relations to Christians, 80
Turkey, world war, 107
Turkistan, Nestorian mission, 64
Tyari and Tikhoma, tribes of, 22

Urhai, Edessa, 24
Uzgeg Khan, 65

Valerian, Emperor, 45

Western Missions, influence of, 89–105
Whal, Rudolph, 104
Wigram, W. A., 100
World War, 107–113
Wu-stung, Emperor, 71

Yahb-Allaha, Patriarch, 67
Yezidis, 22

Zoroaster, prophecy, 24
Zoroastrianism, decline of, 38